"In *Cultural Counterfeits*, Jen
and sensitive issues of our d
biblical insight, and godly compassion. In these pages you will find a winsome call away from the world's false promises and toward what is real, true,
and beautiful."

Nancy Guthrie, Bible teacher; author, *Even Better than Eden*

"Jen Oshman is a clear and trusted voice of wisdom in our current age. She
thinks deeply and biblically about the issues that bombard us—and helps us
to do the same. In *Cultural Counterfeits*, Jen pulls back the curtain to reveal
the empty promises offered by five idols of our day. Jen's words are full of
insight, compassion, and truth. Whether you are combating these lies in your
own soul or coming alongside those you love, this book will expose how the
idols not only fail us, but actually betray and harm us. She then reminds
us that there is ultimately only one who can truly satisfy the longing in our
souls—Jesus, the one in whom all the treasures of wisdom and knowledge
are found."

Courtney Doctor, Coordinator of Women's Initiatives, The Gospel
Coalition; author, *From Garden to Glory* and *Steadfast: A Devotional
Bible Study on the Book of James*

"This book is provocative in all the right ways. Jen Oshman wants to ensure
that women don't settle for less than God's good and glorious intention for
their life. Jen takes on some of the most pressing issues of our day, boldly
proclaiming biblical truth while overflowing with gospel grace that soothes
the sinner's heart and breaks the Pharisee's pride."

Trevin Wax, Vice President of Research and Resource Development,
North American Mission Board; author, *This Is Our Time*

"This is an important and much-needed book. With boldness and wisdom,
Jen thoughtfully unpacks the prevailing cultural lies about what it means to
be a woman and beautifully points to the truth of whom God created us to be.
Cultural Counterfeits strikes the rare balance of grace and truth, and I recom-
mend it to anyone who is tired of the empty promises of this age and is looking
for something lasting."

Vaneetha Rendall Risner, author, *Walking Through Fire: A Memoir of
Loss and Redemption*

"Jen's voice is a herald for believers, equipping us with biblical truth to confront the unsatisfying messages of the world and the damaging lies of our enemy. She proclaims a better message, one full of abundant life in Jesus Christ. *Cultural Counterfeits* is a valuable read for everyone in our churches, whether men and women, young or old."

Tony Merida, Lead Pastor, Imago Dei Church, Raleigh, North Carolina; author, *Ordinary*

"Women are confronted with all sorts of ideas in today's culture. It's hard to know what is true and what truth is to be believed. Jen Oshman unpacks the most common ideas women face with care, research, and a more beautiful vision of God's plan for us. Jen has years of experience as a ministry worker of the gospel, as a student of the word, and as a mom of daughters. As a mom of sons and as someone who ministers to women, I'm thankful for her work! This is a book I plan to give to the women I minister to, and I hope you will do the same."

Courtney Reissig, author, *Teach Me to Feel* and *The Accidental Feminist*

Cultural Counterfeits

Cultural Counterfeits

*Confronting 5 Empty Promises of Our Age and
How We Were Made for So Much More*

Jen Oshman

Foreword by Christine Hoover

CROSSWAY®

WHEATON, ILLINOIS

Library of Congress Cataloging-in-Publication Data

Names: Oshman, Jen, 1978– author.
Title: Cultural counterfeits : confronting 5 empty promises of our age and how we were made for so much more / Jen Oshman.
Description: Wheaton, Illinois : Crossway, 2022. | Includes bibliographical references and index.
Identifiers: LCCN 2021030973 (print) | LCCN 2021030974 (ebook) | ISBN 9781433576324 (trade paperback) | ISBN 9781433576331 (pdf) | ISBN 9781433576348 (mobipocket) | ISBN 9781433576355 (epub)
Subjects: LCSH: Christian women—Religious life. | Identity (Psychology)—Religious aspects—Christianity. | Women—Religious Aspects—Christianity. | Christianity and culture.
Classification: LCC BV4527 .O8548 2022 (print) | LCC BV4527 (ebook) | DDC 248.8/43—dc23
LC record available at https://lccn.loc.gov/2021030973
LC ebook record available at https://lccn.loc.gov/2021030974

For Rebekah, Zoe, Abby Grace, and Hannah
I love you more than words can say. May you know with deep
down joy and hope the "so much more" that you were made for.
There will always, always be a place for you at my table.

Contents

PART 3: WE WERE MADE FOR SO MUCH MORE

Foreword

RECENTLY A YOUNG WOMAN in my church came to me after a Sunday morning service with consternation on her face. She'd recently met a Christian man who lived in a different city, and they'd been getting to know one another primarily by text. She was excited about him, his involvement in his local church, and the possibilities of where dating him might lead.

Somehow, however, the subject of sexual ethics had come up in one of their text conversations. He'd explained to her why he intended to have sex before marriage and why he considered this a God-honored practice.

While I appreciated his candor at such an early stage in their relationship—long before my friend's heart attached to his—I fumed at how he was taking God's name and attaching it to his own selfish agenda. My counsel came swiftly: "Do not question whether your standards are too high. If he's willing to compromise on this and twist God's word in such a way, what else might he be willing to compromise on within marriage? He's told you who he is, and we can thank God for that. Run."

Moments later, several other young, single women joined our conversation. Already aware of the situation their friend faced, they seemed to me both frustrated and unfazed. Curious, I asked them if this—a "trying on" of sexual compatibility before committing to marriage—was a common theme they were hearing among their peers. They nodded and described their disappointment regarding just how much God's perfect and beautiful intentions in creating sex, marriage, and women themselves have been distorted and confused even among God's people.

For the rest of the week, I roiled with righteous anger. I wanted to do or say something to convey the beautiful truth to as many as might listen: God's ways are the best ways! His ways are not only good, they are glorious beyond our comprehension and for our joy. To live by counterfeits is to live an unprofitable, colorless life. To live by counterfeits is not to live at all but rather to die.

Soon after, Jen Oshman put this book in my hands. With counterfeits already on my mind, I devoured her words, thanking God not only for her courage but for her biblical wisdom. We have certainly, as Jen says, found ourselves in a far country. Almost every arena of our lives has been impacted, and it's difficult at times to discern what is true from what is not. However, we must not forget that competing ideas are not equal competitors. There is truth and then there are many iterations of counterfeits to that truth.

Jen, in this book, has spoken the beautiful truth. Let us listen.

Christine Hoover
Author, Podcaster, and Bible Teacher
christinehoover.net

Acknowledgments

THERE'S NOTHING IN MY LIFE—no sphere, no endeavor, no project—that is not a group effort. I am a woman rich with support that I do not deserve. Whether it's in missions overseas, church planting here at home, ministering to women, writing, raising my kids, or loving my husband, I can point to a team of people who pray for me, cheer for me, and hold my arms up high when I am too tired to do so myself. And that's true for this book too. It has been a group effort from the very beginning. These words of thanks feel far from sufficient to communicate the gratitude I feel for each team player.

To our supporters with Pioneers International: thank you for your financial and prayer support for over twenty years. In a very practical way you made this book possible. It is no overstatement to say that we could not serve at home or overseas without your sacrificial partnership.

To my local church, Redemption Parker: it is one of my greatest joys to call you family. Thank you for your enthusiasm, for praying, checking in, bearing my doubts and fears, and valuing my role in our local body as well as in the broader church community. Your support is wind in my sails. I'm especially thankful to the Lord for our extremely supportive elders, the life-giving women's Bible studies I get to be a part of, and to Sandie, Steph, Molly, Christine, and Amanda, for diligently pursuing me as I wrote and lifting up every need and worry in prayer. Tears well up, even now, as I consider how precious RP is to me.

To my partners in ministry in Acts 29 and TGC: many thanks to the countless pastors, pastors' wives, and women in ministry who have voiced encouragement to me. Our broader ministry community has been a well of strength and inspiration. To see how we cheer one another on in this community is a great joy. Kellie and Sara, my local A29 sisters, thank you for checking in so often and always asking how to pray.

To my excellent publishing team: Andrew Wolgemuth, thank you for tirelessly engaging my almost never-ending questions and concerns. I am grateful to call you friend and brother. Dave DeWit, I don't think there's a better champion of women writers out there. I am so grateful for your words of support, practical feedback, and genuine desire to see my efforts succeed. Todd Augustine, thank you for your patience when I wanted to make big changes, your confidence in this final work, and seeing this whole project through. Tara Davis, thank you for your heart for editing. You made this book better with both your skills and your sensitivity.

To my freditors: Shar, Martha, Whitney, Lauren, and MaKayla, thank you for engaging so deeply in this work with me. You all spent hours thinking critically, sharing your insights, correcting my blind spots, and freely giving of your wisdom. I cannot fully convey what a support and relief it was to have your partnership in this work. Thank you for pouring yourselves out. To Carrie, Meghan, Kim, Jen, Kristie, Rachel, and other friends around the globe who prayed and encouraged often, your texts and emails were always the push I needed that very day. Thank you.

To my family: Mom, there is much of you here. Thank you for instilling in me a desire to read, think, and write deeply. Mark, you are my partner in every way. You have given this project so much. How can I ever thank you for weathering all of the highs and lows of this work? And you weathered them with joy, steadiness, and nothing but confidence in me and God's call and equipping in me. I love you. Rebekah, Zoe, Abby Grace, and Hannah, you girls were a constant source of imagination and gravity to me as I wrote. Thank you for humoring countless conversations about these topics with me. You teach me so much. I love you.

Finally, to my Father in heaven. I have sinned against heaven and against you. And yet, you watched for me while I was still a long way off. You ran to me, embraced me with compassion, and lavished me with your love. Thank you for inviting me to your feast.

Introduction

I, LIKE YOU, want to be accepted. I want the approval and applause of others. I hate to cause conflict or to offend. I like it when other people like me.

But these are polarizing days, and complete acceptance is hard to come by. Most of us—whether we're in a classroom, a boardroom, a coffee shop, or online—keep a low profile and keep as quiet as we can, so as to not be seen as arrogant or rude. We want to *be* genuinely humble and kind, and we want to be *perceived* so too.

That's what's hard about this book. I am well aware that some parts will offend both the secular and the spiritual, both the deconstructed and the Christian, both the younger brother and the older one. And I don't like that. I don't want to offend.

So why take time to call out our cultural counterfeits anyway? Why critique the empty promises of our age rather than lie low? Why potentially offend both those who are in the world and those who are in the church?

Because Jesus is the way and the truth and the life. No one can be saved, and no one can thrive, apart from him. He is our one and only hope. And so many of us have misplaced our hope in the counterfeits of our age.

Jesus's acceptance of us, on his terms, is infinitely and eternally more valuable than our acceptance of one another.

The gospel is not *only* that we are sinners in need of a Savior. The gospel starts with a good Creator who's been pursuing us since even before we gave in to sin. If you and I are going to be well, we have to *know him*. We have to know and abide by the character and design and purposes of our Creator and Savior. Without him we have nothing—nothing of substance, nothing eternal, nothing to hold on to in the chaos and in our pain.

The counterfeits of our age are a deviation from what our good God intends, a marring of the good gifts he offers us. As God asks us to love him and to love others, we do that by pointing ourselves and our loved ones back to him. He is the hope for our hurting world.

Embracing a Jesus-is-the-only-way perspective is costly for sure. It might cost us friendships, professional opportunities, and finances. But, to use the apostle Peter's words, "Lord, to whom shall we go? You have the words of eternal life, and we have believed, and have come to know, that you are the Holy One of God" (John 6:68–69).

Jesus alone is the Holy One of God, and he alone has the words of eternal life. What else would we believe? Who else would we trust? Who else would we offer up to others?

The warm, true, and hard words of Jesus have been wooing people to himself for millennia, and that's not going to stop now. Our God is not freaking out. He is not anxious. He is not worried about offending, because for those who have ears to hear, his word speaks life. As values and what's normal and permissible and celebrated in the twenty-first century change, Jesus's words do not.

He is an anchor in the storm. A constant in a sea of change. An enduring refuge when it's hard to know up from down. And as you and I who follow Jesus hold out the word of truth, we will be like stars shining in a dark universe (Phil. 2:15).

Our homes and our hearts will hold out hope when our neighbors and loved ones are exhausted from trying to keep up with the idols of our age. The warm steadiness of Christ-followers will be a porch light in the dark night. Our lives—as countercultural and embarrassing and awkward as they may be—will point to Jesus, who says, "Come to me, all who labor and are heavy laden, and I will give you rest" (Matt. 11:28).

So read on and cling to Christ because it's his acceptance that matters most. Read on because you, like me, believe he came that we might be saved through him alone. Jesus is the way. He is the truth. He is the life. Christian, as you follow Jesus, *you offer life*.

PART 1

YOU ARE HERE

We live in a unique moment that was delivered to us by a specific timeline in history. Part 1 explores how we got here, focusing especially on the ideas that led up to and came out of the Sexual Revolution. As we seek to understand where we are on the map of history, we'll also be reminded of God's word, which is a timeless lens through which we can view changing trends.

> The God who made the world and everything in it, being Lord of heaven and earth, does not live in temples made by man, nor is he served by human hands, as though he needed anything, since he himself gives to all mankind life and breath and everything. And he made from one man every nation of mankind to live on all the face of the earth, having determined allotted periods and the boundaries of their dwelling place, that they should seek God, and perhaps feel their way toward him and find him. (Acts 17:24–27)

1

Waking Up in a Far Country

WHEN I WAS FOUR YEARS OLD, I ran away from home. I packed my mom's twenty-year-old 1960s American Tourister cosmetic suitcase with all the essentials and announced, "I don't like it here," to my parents, who were preparing dinner in the kitchen. To my surprise they didn't come after me. So I marched down the street and into the sunset.

When I had made it about four houses down, probably to my friend Colin's house, which was the extent of my comfort zone, I began to shiver. It was a chilly Colorado evening. I hadn't packed a sweater, so I did what every four-year-old in this situation does: I went back home. My mom greeted me with a smile. Dinner was ready, and I sat down with my family to eat.

I know I'm not alone in this memory. I suspect you did this too. Is there an American child who hasn't had a rebellious moment and thought *I can do better on my own*? Autonomy is in our DNA. From birth we're a pioneering people who buck up against boundaries and suspect the grass is greener on the other side of just about every fence we see.

We come by it honestly, though. Consider our first parents, Adam and Eve, in the garden of Eden. God created the first man and first woman and set them in the midst of his good creation. There were fish in the sea, birds in the heavens, and livestock over all the earth. There were plants and trees and seedlings and all kinds of vegetation. The sun and the moon and the stars shone. It was all very good. God blessed Adam and Eve, told them to be fruitful and multiply, and instructed them to cultivate all the living things he had made (Gen. 1:28).

They had much freedom and just one boundary: "You may surely eat of every tree of the garden, but of the tree of the knowledge of good and evil you shall not eat, for in the day that you eat of it you shall surely die" (Gen. 2:16–17). The crafty serpent came along and questioned this one-and-only limitation. "Did God really say that? You will not surely die," he assured Adam and Eve (see Gen. 3:2, 4).

Convinced that God's plan was not, in fact, best, that they knew at least a little bit better, Adam and Eve went ahead and took that fateful bite. You know the rest of the story. God sent them out of the garden, and we've been east of Eden ever since (Gen. 3:23–24).

This is our way. It has been our condition since that first bite. In our fallen state we think we know best, that we can do better. And so we continuously set out to make our best lives happen right now.

The serpent isn't very creative, but he is consistent. Millennia and generations after the garden he keeps asking you and me, *Did God really say that? You will not surely die. Go ahead and try it.* And like four-year-old me, we so often do. We set out from home, we leave safe boundaries and good gifts, and we try to create a better life with our own hands and in our own way.

Two Stories in Our Heads

Here's how this looks in the twenty-first century. In his podcast *The Living Temple*, author and pastor Mark Sayers says there are two stories running around in all of our heads.[1] The two stories are largely subconscious. They're the subtle background music moving us to make the choices we make day in and day out.

The first story is broadcast loudly across pop culture, social media, and all media. It proclaims that you and I are the center of the universe. We are unique individuals, and we can be awesome. We just need to create our identities. By making the right choices with our wardrobes and weekends, and by hanging out with the right people and doing the right things, we can be limitlessly happy. The world offers you and me an amazing life; we just have to go out and make it happen.

The second story is quiet. It's more of a whisper from the back burner in our brains, but it refuses to be silenced. It will not go away. It's there in the quiet, in the middle of the night, when the new novelty doesn't measure up or the relationship breaks rather than binds. It's the questioning and the longing when the over-promises of the first story underdeliver. The whisper tells us we were made for more. In a hushed voice it insists that we have an immoveable and important identity, a sort of real home somewhere out there. We're longing for it, and we know it's not just in our imaginations. *There's got to be more to this life*, it nags.

We continuously suppress that second story, though—largely because the first story is so loud. It's hard to argue with. Everything from Instagram to movies to clothing ads to political campaigns

1   Mark Sayers, "This Is for People Who Want to Go Deep," May 8, 2019, in *The Living Temple*, podcast, https://rebuilders.co/podcasts/the-living-temple-s1/ep1.

to Supreme Court decisions declares that we can be whoever we want to be.

Pursuing the second story would take time and intentionality. It would require going against just about every cultural grain. It would mean rejecting the societal song that says you can have your best life right now. It would mean weaning off the dopamine hits we get from shopping for our best selves. It would mean believing there's a real truth out there that we must discover, rather than thinking we are the makers of our own truth, right here, right now.

We are a people prone to shopping for new shoes, new partners, new orientations, and new careers with each changing season. We rarely, if ever, question the first story. It's so taken for granted that we don't wonder at overworking or consumer debt or gender fluidity. These are all things we have to do—to at least try or try on—to see if they're the right fit to finally make us truly happy.

It's a tale as old as we are. It's the serpent who keeps saying *If you really want to live, take matters into your own hands. Take a bite here, or there. It surely won't hurt you. Did God really say that? Your life can be better, just keep biting, keep sampling.*

The Burnout Generation

If we're honest, though, we know our pursuit of the first story isn't going well. The cultural cacophony says keep running harder, and boy, are we trying. But this race has no end. There's no real satisfaction to be had, because there's no real finish line. Under duress we keep going and keep hoping, but we're exhausted.

The exhaustion experienced is well documented. It's called burnout. Burnout is more than stress or anxiety. It's a hopelessness that leads to isolation and disengagement from work or school, friends and family. It's a weariness that won't let up and a cynicism that settles in. Burnout keeps people from accomplishing their normal routines, from feeling settled in their skin. Burnout doesn't give way to the usual pick-me-ups.

Sociologists and economists have been noting for years that while burnout happens to all of us, millennials are especially prone. The World Health Organization even labeled millennial burnout a medical condition. And a national psychiatric survey says 96 percent of millennials feel it on a daily basis.[2]

Psychoanalyst Josh Cohen provides a helpful take on the condition. He says, "The message that we can work harder and be better at everything — even rest and relaxation! — results in a strange composite of exhaustion and anxiety, a permanent state of dissatisfaction with who we are and what we have. And it leaves us feeling that we are servants rather than masters of our work — and not just of our waged employment, but of the unending work we put into achieving our so-called best selves."[3]

The disconnection between the first story and the second story—the idea that we can create our best selves and the reality that we aren't arriving at the destination we had envisioned—has us exhausted and anxious. Identity crises abound, not just for millennials, but for all of us in the twenty-first century. This is burnout. Not just with work, but with play, with our identities and relationships and plans and dreams and everything.

Modern Label, Age-Old Problem

Here's why we're burned out: we're making a massive mistake about reality. That second, quiet, nagging story is *true*. But we're living

2   Jaimy Ford, "Why Do 96% of Millennials Experience Burnout?," Bud to Boss (website), https://www.budtoboss.com/.
3   Josh Cohen, "Millennial Burnout Is Real, but It Touches a Serious Nerve with Critics. Here's Why," *Think* column on *NBC News*, February 23, 2019, https://www.nbcnews.com/think/.

like it's not. There really is more to this life, but it can't be found in our own conjuring, our own identity creation and curation.

Burnout is a new label, but it's not a new condition. It's a new take on the age-old problem of idolatry.

When you think of an idol, you probably think of some kind of statue that is believed to have power. You might think of fertility goddesses at the history museum or Hindu gods and goddesses increasingly popular here in the West. And while these are certainly idols, the definition doesn't stop there. Author and pastor Timothy Keller says, "An idol is whatever you look at and say, in your heart of hearts, 'If I have that, then I'll feel my life has meaning, then I'll know I have value, then I'll feel significant and secure.'"[4]

Idols are counterfeits. Idolatry is when we ascribe meaning or power to something that cannot actually bear it—when we expect created, temporary things to deliver that which only the one true God can. It's as old as Adam and Eve. It's not just millennials who are tempted by idols; it's anyone living and breathing in the twenty-first century. No one of any age is immune.

We set up these idols in our hearts and give them meaning and power that should be reserved for God alone (Ezek. 14:3). We deify them by making them central to our lives, our value, our identity, and our purpose. We can make idols out of partners, children, careers, politics, money, sex, power, clothes, homes, vacations, cars, and who-knows-what else. The sky is the limit, really, because, as John Calvin wrote, "Man's nature, so to speak, is a perpetual factory of idols."[5]

---

4   Timothy Keller, *Counterfeit Gods: The Empty Promises of Money, Sex, and Power, and the Only Hope That Matters* (New York: Dutton, 2009), xviii.
5   John Calvin, *Institutes of the Christian Religion*, ed. John T. McNeill, trans. Ford Lewis Battles (Philadelphia: Westminster, 1960), 1.11.8.

Your heart and mine are idol factories. We can make an idol out of anything.

Harmony with Reality

Theologian Dallas Willard says idolatry is "an error at the 'world-view' level. It arises from the crying need of human beings to gain control over their lives. That need is understandable, of course, and it must be met in some way. But idolatry tries to meet the need by assigning powers to an object of human imagination and artifice, powers that object does not actually possess."[6]

We are suffering because we are living outside of reality, and "reality does not adjust itself to accommodate our false beliefs."[7] It's just not real—it's not realistic, it's not real life—that anything temporary like sex or another human being or any consumer item on Amazon will fulfill our deep-down longings, dreams, and desires. This is an age-old truth: the fruit in the garden of Eden overpromised and underdelivered, and the idols in our lives do too.

Reality is stubborn like that. It won't go well with us if we refuse to live according to what's real. The serpent tricked Adam and Eve, and he tricks us today too. We can pretend and invent and hope against hope all day long. But we suffer when our expectations are not grounded in what's real.

Human well-being requires harmony with reality.

Sayers says we imbue fleeting and fragile things with godlike power so that we can feel safe. We want to control our lives and outcomes, so we use the idols of our age to bring about the results we're looking for. But they end up controlling us because we keep

6   Dallas Willard, *Knowing Christ Today: Why We Can Trust Spiritual Knowledge* (New York: Harper Collins, 2009), 41.

7   Willard, *Knowing Christ Today*, 39.

looking to them, making offerings to them, putting our hope in them. But they never really deliver. They never fully satisfy.

When our idols don't deliver—when they disappoint, when we realize we've been used rather than us using them—what if we instead turn to where we are truly loved and treasured without condition and beyond our comprehension?

What if burnout is a gift of God, calling us home? To him. To the love of our Father.

The Prodigal Son

Jesus tells the story of the prodigal son in Luke 15. You might know it well. A man has two sons, and the younger son asks for his share of the inheritance while the father is still alive. The father gives it to him, the son gathers all he has, and then heads out into a far country where he "squander[s] his property in reckless living" (Luke 15:13). A famine strikes, and he finds himself penniless. So he hires himself out to a man in the foreign country, who gives him the job of feeding pigs in his fields. The younger son is so broke and destitute that he longs to eat the pigs' food, but "no one [gives] him anything" (Luke 15:16).

We are not unlike this son, are we? We've been given an inheritance—so many good things by our Father in heaven—and yet we take them and run off to a far country. We seek the kingdoms of this world and their glory. Leaving our Father and home behind, we believe the universe is all about us and we can be awesome by curating the right experiences and identities.

And like the Prodigal Son, we find ourselves hungry, unsatisfied, longing for more. This is burnout. This is what idolatry delivers.

The son's misery finally brings him to himself (Luke 15:17). He hits rock bottom. He's done chasing that first story. He reasons that even his father's servants are better off than he is. He rises up, determines to return to his father, admits his wrong thinking and wrongdoing, and seeks to at least earn his keep as a hired servant on his father's land.

The Bible tells us while the son is still a long way off, his father sees him and feels compassion. He runs and embraces his son and kisses him (Luke 15:20). The son hardly gets through his apology before the father tells the servants to clothe him, kill the fattened calf, and prepare a celebration for the son's return (Luke 15:22–23).

The son finds that the second story really is true. He really was made for more than reckless living, more than feeding pigs in a foreign land. He was made to receive the lavish love and provision of his father. He was made for the feast at home, for the celebration of his homecoming.

Prodigal Daughters

In our day, the far country remains, and it's just as alluring to us as it was to the Prodigal Son. We too gather our things and head out, hoping to discover ourselves somewhere out there. The Western world after the Sexual Revolution parades especially winsome and convincing idols before women and girls.

These idols promise empowerment and freedom, but instead deliver exploitation and enslavement. *You can be awesome*, they say, *if you'll just give yourself over to this identity, this way of life.*

There are many far countries, many idols of course, but a handful have proven to be the most enticing and the most destructive of our age. There's the idol of outward beauty. It applauds the young, the strong, and the visually pleasing, but it despises and twists true human beauty. Then there's the idol of sex. Convinced that sex is our deepest need and highest good, we hook up over and over but never find real soul satisfaction. The idol of abortion is in cahoots with hooking up, promising us control, choice, and self-determination. And then there's the newer but tenacious far country of LGBTQIA+, promising a home to any girl wrestling with who she is and what she feels.

These cultural counterfeits, or far countries, or idols, appear so shiny, so promising, so life-giving. They've been wildly successful at drawing us in. But they've inflicted so much harm. We're now out in the foreign fields, with the pigs, so hungry we'd eat anything.

May we come to ourselves. May we rise up and go. The Father is watching and waiting even now, eager to give us compassion, love, forgiveness, and a truly soul-satisfying feast.

Older Brother, Older Sisters

The Prodigal Son has an older brother, as you may know, and we can't leave him out. When he realizes his younger brother has returned and a celebration is underway, he is angry and refuses to go in (Luke 15:28). His father goes out to him (just as he went out to the younger son), and the older son protests, "Look, these many years I have served you, and I never disobeyed your command, yet you never gave me a young goat, that I might celebrate with my friends. But when this son of yours came, who has devoured your property with prostitutes, you killed the fattened calf for him!'" (Luke 15:29–30). The father replies, "Son, you are always with me, and all that is mine is yours" (Luke 15:31).

Both sons sought the good life through idolatry. One is more obvious than the other. The younger brother's reckless living is more shocking, seemingly more egregious. But the older brother too fell into idolatry. He placed his hope and trust in his own good behavior. He depended on his right choices to deliver the good life.

This idol wreaks havoc, even now, in our Christian circles. Perhaps in an effort to counter our crude age, or perhaps because we're sinful humans and inevitably drawn to either license or legalism, we've set up an idol of purity, marriage, and motherhood. Unwittingly, we've exalted these good gifts above the giver. These good gifts, though, are no less idolatrous if we look at them and say, "If I have that, then I'll feel my life has meaning, then I'll know I have value, then I'll feel significant and secure."[8]

We see ourselves in the younger brother and the older brother. The brothers in this parable are all too familiar, all too relatable.

There's Very Good News; but First, the Bad

Here's the very good news that I can hardly wait to get to after we seek understanding of our own age and idols: in both cases, the father goes out to both sons, lavishes love and forgiveness, and invites them in to feast with him. Whether you are languishing and starving in a far country or steeped in your own moralism and no less dissatisfied, the Father is watching and waiting. As we come to ourselves, God stands ready to run out and embrace us, and to invite us in to the feast he has prepared for you and me.

Let's have the faith of a child—the faith of four-year-old me, who knew she could turn around and go back home. May the mercy, peace, and goodness of our God be the backdrop to every word you read on the pages ahead.

In chapter 2 we'll look at how we got here. The Western world after the Sexual Revolution is a battlefield for women and girls. We need to know that a specific history delivered us into this moment. In chapter 3 we'll look at how the Bible is a timeless and reliable

---

8 Keller, *Counterfeit Gods*, xviii.

road map for our age. It really is good news for women and girls, as it points us to what's true, what's real and everlasting, that we might live in harmony with reality and our God. He is for us.

Part 2 will unpack the most attractive and sinister counterfeits of our age: outward beauty and ability, cheap sex, abortion, the LGBTQIA+ spectrum, and a twisted view of marriage and motherhood. With anecdotes and plenty of sociological research you and I will see how they've overpromised and underdelivered. We'll look beyond their boastful facades and see the real destruction underneath.

Finally, after looking these idols in the face in part 2, part 3 will reorient us to how good and sovereign and kind our God is. Part 3 is meant to be a worship-inducing, joy-giving conclusion. My hope is to lift our eyes up off of what can be a discouraging cultural landscape and onto God's goodness. In chapter 9 we'll look at ten reasons the Bible shows us it's good to be a girl, and in chapter 10 we will be overwhelmed by God's love and mercy and the feast he's preparing for you and me.

By the end of this book, I pray your heart and eyes will be fixed on Jesus who—as a truer, better, ultimate older brother in our story—makes a way for you and me and every woman and girl to come home. By his blood we can be reconciled to the Father. No matter what we've done, he's not afraid to call us brothers and sisters (Heb. 2:11).

One word of caution before we go on. The content in this book will at times be especially difficult to read if you have personally endured trauma at the hands of any of these idols. There may be research or anecdotes that are triggering for you. Consider reading this book with a trusted friend or group of women whom you can rely on to help you pursue healing and wholeness as you confront these empty promises head-on. Find friends who love Jesus, Christian counseling, support groups, and any other means of healing. You are not alone, and God's desire for you is to walk in complete freedom.

My hope is that we will be well, that we will find life. We've been so sick for so long, giving ourselves over to the empty promises of our age. We've been lied to, and we've believed. But God made us for so much more. If human well-being requires harmony with reality, then let's look at what's real, what's true, what's genuinely good and beautiful, so that we might be well, so that we might truly live.

Discussion Questions

1. Did you ever run away as a kid, like I did as a four-year-old? Share the story with the others in your group.

2. Can you relate to the two stories that are running around in our heads? The first story says you can be awesome, you just have to make it happen. The second story whispers there must be more to this life. Give an example of how you try to make your life awesome—where you seek to conjure up your own identity. And give an example of a time when you suspected that you were made for so much more.

3. Tim Keller says, "An idol is whatever you look at and say, in your heart of hearts, 'If I have that, then I'll feel my life has meaning, then I'll know I have value, then I'll feel significant and secure.'" What idols do you see being especially attractive in your sphere?

4. Read the parable of the prodigal son in Luke 15:11–32. Which brother do you immediately identify with?

5. Does adhering to and offering the words of Jesus in our world excite you or scare you? Why?

6. Close by praying for the Lord to reveal his merciful and loving Father's heart to you in the coming chapters and weeks as you read through this book. Pray that God would help you to love his word and his truth, so that you might shine like stars in the universe, holding fast the word of life (Phil. 2:15–16).

2

The Sexual Revolution
Meets #MeToo

RED CLOAKS AND WHITE BONNETS have made a comeback. The Puritan-era look is now a mainstream public statement for women's rights. When we see women wearing the cloaks and bonnets and standing in groups on the street or at the Capitol, we know what they're out there for. They're donning the costume of *The Handmaid's Tale*, a Hulu adaptation of Margaret Atwood's novel by the same name, and they've shown up to, among other things, support Planned Parenthood, denounce sexist policies or politicians, or cry #MeToo.

The television version of *The Handmaid's Tale* swept the Emmys and won a couple of Golden Globes in its first season. The plot conveys a dystopian future in the United States in which a theocratic government imposes a sick characterization of a fundamentalist Christian regime on the people. In order to increase the country's population, fertile women are enslaved—they are made to be handmaids—to bear children. The show has "decidedly biblical overtones"[1] and obviously resonates with a significant portion of the American public.

The handmaids' message is clear: when theology and government mix, women are literally or figuratively enslaved and exploited. Christianity, they proclaim, is bad for women.

Even if the sight of the costumes is jolting, the handmaids' views are not extreme in today's context. This narrative is in our water. I remember as a teen mocking a male relative (behind his back) who had joined a Christian men's group that supported his role as a husband and father. It seemed laughable to me that a Christian group believed they could help him treat his wife better. Didn't Christian groups do the opposite? I was even a Christian at the time, but somehow the idea that Christianity denigrates women was securely lodged in my mind. Even now I regularly get questions from Christian women who quietly wonder if this is a skeleton in our closet. Does Christianity want to keep us down?

Is the way forward for women in the West to move further away from Christianity? Should we join our American sisters in red cloaks and white bonnets to put down our faith and stand up for ourselves?

The Gender Gap in Christianity

The notion that Christian leaders have always been wealthy white men and they've used their faith and position to keep women down is widely assumed and almost unquestioned in the West. Global bestsellers like *The DaVinci Code* reinforce our suspicion that Christianity has a secret origin wherein men assembled the Bible in such a way as to silence female voices and rid the church of female influence. Never mind that such books and narratives

1   Brett McCracken, "Hollywood Is as God-Haunted as Ever," The Gospel Coalition, October 7, 2017, https://www.thegospelcoalition.org/.

are without a historical basis. The conspiracies are just too enticing and have captured the imaginations of many.

But here's what's actually, strikingly true: in the United States, in the West, and around the globe, more women than men are Christian.[2] *Christianity is predominantly female.* And that's the way it has always been.

Jesus Christ's life, death, and resurrection initiated a cultural rumble that became a revolution in the Greco-Roman world. In a first-century setting fixated on power, Jesus came on the scene promising blessing, heaven, and inheritance to the poor, to those who mourn, and to the meek. In a culture soaked in violence, Jesus called his followers to love God, to love others, and to love even their enemies.

This care of humanity, this selfless elevation of others, set the early Christians far apart from their pagan contemporaries. Whereas the pagan gods required payment and sacrifice but promised nothing in return, the Christian God—in the person of Jesus—made his love for humans unmistakable and asked them to go and do likewise. Believing that heaven awaits and eternity matters, the first Christians were emboldened to care for the sick during epidemics, welcome the foreigner and the outcast, feed the poor, and comfort the afflicted.

And no one felt this more than women "because within the Christian subculture women enjoyed far higher status than did women in the Greco-Roman world at large."[3] In the early centuries in Rome, female infanticide was widely practiced (discarding baby girls in trash heaps in preference for baby boys), families often gave

---

2 "The Gender Gap in Religion around the World," Pew Research Center, March 22, 2016, https://www.pewforum.org/.

3 Rodney Stark, *The Rise of Christianity: A Sociologist Reconsiders History* (Princeton: Princeton University Press, 1996), 95.

their girls over to marriage before puberty, girls had no say in who they married and consummation was expected, and once they were married, fidelity was required of the wives, while husbands were encouraged to pursue extramarital sex with both female and male prostitutes.[4]

Christianity stood in stark contrast, elevating marriage, families, and procreation. Christian families allowed their daughters to have a voice in who they married, and they married at much older ages. In Christianity women and girls enjoyed protection from divorce, incest, infidelity, polygamy, child marriage, abortion, infanticide, and mistreatment at the hands of their husbands. Not only that, but Christian women were respected in the church, welcomed in to serve in various capacities and to collaborate in ministry.[5] Following in the footsteps of Jesus, who laid down his life for others, the early Christians gave themselves over to caring for the weak, including babies, women, and all the marginalized.

All of this is not to say that the expression of the Christian church has been faultless throughout history. Healthy church leaders acknowledge the church's shortcomings and the reality that Christianity has been wrongly used for misogynistic ends at certain times. However, the true expression of Christian faith is clearly and rightly seen in these examples from the early church. Selflessness, service, and the elevation of women marked true Christian doctrine and practice in the first century, and it still does today in the twenty-first century.

This is a key reason Christianity is predominantly female: women are cherished, protected, and elevated beyond secular standards. When that doesn't happen, it's a deviation from the true faith.

4   Stark, *The Rise of Christianity*, 105, 117.
5   Stark, *The Rise of Christianity*, 105, 109.

The *Imago Dei*

Sociologist and historian Rodney Stark says that what Christianity gave its early converts was their humanity.[6] The elevation of human life was a bright light in a dark setting. This flows from the Judeo-Christian doctrine of the *imago dei*, the image of God, which Christians still believe is intrinsic in every human.

The opening pages of the Bible say, "God created man in his own image, / in the image of God he created him; / male and female he created them" (Gen. 1:27). Right away, in the very first chapter of Scripture, we see what the Christian church, as well as ages of Jews, have believed: there is a God and he made us. Not only that, but he made us in his image, *imago dei*, and he made us male and female.

For millennia there has been a historic consensus throughout Western civilization that our lives are not accidents or without intention. For ages we have believed we are made in a specific way and for a specific purpose. Up until very recently belief in God has been assumed, respected, and unchallenged. Today, though, we Westerners increasingly reject the idea of a design and a Designer.

They don't know it, but this rejection of a divine author who has authority is the hidden root of what the handmaids in red cloaks and white bonnets are protesting. Indeed, protesting the mistreatment of women is a worthy endeavor, as women endure real harm in many places in our society. This book is itself a protest, a declaration that all is not well and women deserve better. But what the protestors do not grasp is that it's our society-wide distancing from God that has led to our devaluing of the *imago dei* in women and in one another. Protestors feel the devaluing, but they don't know where it comes from. They don't know the source of our value in

6   Stark, *The Rise of Christianity*, 215.

the first place. My hope is that in the pages ahead we can find our way back to that immovable and unshakable source—the God who made us and dignifies us.

First-Wave Feminism

While the handmaids are the most recent iteration in a long line of women who have marched for equality, it would be a mistake to think that they have much in common with the first women who marched. In truth, they see the world very differently than the first feminists.

There's a wide range of feelings about feminism amongst today's Christian women, and for good reason. Feminism has a mixed and shady history. So I'll start by stating where I stand: the genesis of feminism was good and even godly, but the movement took a wrong turn in the 1960s, and since then it has been detrimental, even deadly, to women and girls.

First-wave feminism was, in part, a bold Christian movement that started with, of all things, Prohibition. Starting in the mid-1800s, with the rise of industrialization, long factory hours, in-humane working conditions, and the growth of the urban poor, men turned to strong alcohol for relief. A variety of organizations formed in response, including the Women's Christian Temperance Union, as women sought to protect one another and their children from the drunkenness sweeping the country.

Historian and author Daniel Okrent says, "Men would go to the tavern, drink away mortgage money, drink so much they couldn't go to work the next day, beat their wives, abuse their children. That's what launched the beginning of the temperance movement."[7]

7   Olivia B. Waxman, "The Surprisingly Complex Link between Prohibition and Women's Rights," *Time*, January 18, 2019, https://time.com/.

Women who were not yet allowed to vote or own property and had few options for protecting themselves and their children rose up against this injustice. They sought the right to vote in an effort to protect the marginalized.

The first-wave feminists put biblical truth on display by insisting that women and children are created in the image of God, *imago dei*, and worthy of protection. They rightly marched to vote, to hold property and protect the money they earned, to exercise their gifts and skills in wider society. Amongst them were slavery abolitionists too, insisting on the *imago dei* in African Americans. These activists rightly proclaimed the Christian view that women, children, and people of color are designed by God for good purposes, and society as a whole benefits when they are all invited to the table.

When Sexual Privacy Became Sexual Primacy

While much of the genesis of feminism was good and godly, it tragically went awry in the 1960s. Like so many ideologies in the Western world, it was rooted in biblical truth, but then it left that truth behind. While first-wave feminism was yoked to the theology of the *imago dei*, second-wave feminism yoked itself to the 1960s counterculture and promised self-fulfillment in free love, in throwing off tradition, including—or especially—anything Christian. Everything from conventional genders, relationships, ideas, roles, and families was not only called into question, but seen as oppressive, backward, and even the invention of powerful men to keep vulnerable women in place.

Liberating women in civic life, the workforce, and academics was equated with liberating women in sex and relationships too. Limited roles in society were equated with limited roles in sexuality—both oppressive. It was then that second-wave feminists decreed that the genders had to be the *same* to be equal. Equality was defined as *sameness*. This is the wrong turn that makes modern feminism deadly, which we will further explore in part 2.

The reigning thought in the 1960s and 1970s was, if men can have careers, then so can women, and if men can have sex without bearing babies, then so can women. Preference was given to avoiding or ending pregnancy, rather than anticipating it and celebrating it.

The male body was normed over the female body.

The Supreme Court joined the revolution in *Griswold v. Connecticut* in 1965, citing *a right to sexual privacy* in the Constitution, which one cannot imagine was actually intended by the Founding Fathers. The case granted married Americans access to birth control, which in the twenty-first century sounds blasé, but it's actually revolutionary in and of itself. The advent of birth control meant that sex was no longer for procreation, and it would soon mean that it was no longer just for married men and women. Birth control opened huge floodgates, which we'll look at more in the coming chapters.

It seems unbelievable now, but up until this decision, sex wasn't private. Laws were in place that reenforced millennia-long convictions that sex should be confined to a lifelong commitment between one man and one woman, because sex produces children, and children deserve the peace and protection of a stable family. Lawmakers believed that children deserved to know and receive the love and care of both of their parents for their entire childhood, so things like adultery and cohabitation were illegal. The goal wasn't to suppress adults, but to protect children.

Borrowing capital from first-century Christianity, sexual ethics up until the Sexual Revolution was concerned primarily with procreation and children.

The 1965 *Griswold* decision set a precedent for seeking sexual privacy in future cases: in *Eisenstadt v. Baird* (1972) access to birth control was granted to unmarried couples; in *Roe v. Wade* (1973) abortion was legalized across the country; in *Carey v. Population Services International* (1977) access to birth control was granted to juveniles; in *Lawrence v. Texas* (2003) homosexuality was legalized; and in *Obergefell v. Hodges* (2015) same-sex marriage was enshrined in law.

In the Sexual Revolution sex was made central, primary. Sexual ethics morphed from protecting the *imago dei* and especially the vulnerable (or at least attempting to), into "do whatever feels good and get what you can." Self-fulfillment through sex. Personal pleasure over protection of others.

Our sisters in red cloaks and white bonnets march precisely because this elevation of individual autonomy over communal good has been harmful.

The Great Scattering

Also at play since the 1960s has been the Great Scattering. Coined by sociologist Mary Ebberstadt, the Great Scattering is simply the breakup of the family. Ebberstadt says we've scattered because of "the widespread social changes that followed the technological shock of the birth control pill . . . the de-stigmatization of non-marital sex in all its varieties, and a sharp rise in behaviors [such as] abortion, fatherless homes, family shrinkage, family breakup, and other phenomena that have become commonplace in the world since the 1960s."[8]

Most Westerners think these massive shifts in how we live are a net positive. In the pursuit of self, we think increased emancipation from everything spells unending freedom. And we love freedom.

---

8   Mary Ebberstadt, *Primal Screams: How the Sexual Revolution Created Identity Politics* (West Conshohocken, PA: Templeton Press, 2019), 9.

Consent is now our only boundary, our only law, because the autonomous self takes priority over the common good. The only impediment to our individual freedom, at least for now, is the consent of another, if another is involved. Consent, though, is flimsy and subjective, and we often see today how it doesn't always bear up under the needs of the giver or receiver.

Things have radically changed in a very short amount of time. For millennia in the West we were after our communal good, what's best for children, how to keep families together, how to protect the *imago dei* in each other, partly by virtue and partly by the necessarily communal nature of premodern life. We didn't do it perfectly, but there was an agreed-upon virtue, at least. We enjoyed strength, safety, and stability from strong and central social frameworks.

But in just this lifetime we have thrown all of that off, thinking *self is best*. What's crazy and shocking, though, is that we've inadvertently, but greatly, harmed ourselves in the process.

Girls Have Lost So Much

The dissolution of our families has been uniquely awful for girls. It has skewed our views of the opposite gender and messed with the way we view ourselves.

As our families have scattered, we have lost watching our dads and moms interact, love each other, hurt each other, and forgive each other. We've lost the witness of fierce commitment and humility. We've lost having a dad at home to teach us how it feels to be respected by a man who really cares. We've lost siblings and cousins and neighborhoods where boys and girls run amok and figure out how to be friends with the opposite gender. We've lost protective brothers and other boys who don't sexualize us but relate to us in wholesome ways.

46

The thing about revolutions is that they change everything. And the Sexual Revolution sexualized everything. It brought sex front and center, labeled it our greatest desire, our highest good, the best way to fulfill self.

So rather than digging in and making marriage work, husbands and wives leave each other and seek gratification elsewhere. Rather than pursuing lifelong and emotionally intimate relationships, we seek sex without strings. Rather than view one another as wholly human, we see each other—and ourselves—as physical bodies in need of a release.

The unforeseen result is that the Sexual Revolution didn't empower women; it silenced them.

It forced women and girls into a societal mold that portrayed powerful and successful women as sexy and sexualized. It transformed women into objects to be consumed, and it required women and girls to say they *liked it*, to conform and agree that sexualization was somehow for our good, our freedom, our elevation. We were so silenced, in fact, that it took a global movement in 2017 for us to find our voices.

#MeToo

The #MeToo movement is a bold indictment that the Sexual Revolution has not been for our good. The red cloaks and white bonnets say as much. Their protests reveal that much of the progress of the last several decades has actually been violent, heinous, and heartbreaking for women.

The #MeToo hashtag gained notoriety in 2017 when women throughout Hollywood began to come forward with allegations of sexual assault, abuse, and rape against film producer Harvey Weinstein. But *Me Too* was a phrase and movement originally coined by

African American activist Taranna Burke in 2006. Burke used the phrase to encourage women and girls to come forward with their own stories of sexual assault and abuse.

The phrase itself betrays recent Western values, portraying the sheer normalcy of sexual violence committed against women and girls. *You were assaulted? Me too.* A recent study reveals that 77 percent of women have been verbally sexually harassed, 51 percent have endured unwelcome sexual touching, and 27 percent have been sexually assaulted.[9]

The 2017 #MeToo movement was painful and revealing. Trusted names, brotherly and fatherly figures, were exposed for who they really are. I grew up with *The Cosby Show*. When my parents were divorcing, Claire and Cliff Huxtable weren't. They were an anchor, an example of family ties and self-sacrificing love. But now I know that Bill Cosby was a serial rapist and all was not well, even if no one said so at the time.

Here's the great irony of our age: "The revolution has made sex itself more ubiquitous than ever before. But it has also estranged men and women as never before, both by shrinking the family and by increasing the mistrust between men and women thanks to widespread consumerism."[10]

Sex is now pervasive but intimacy is elusive. We're in a crisis of trust, of truly valuing one another, of actually caring about what's best for the other person in our beds, not to mention thinking deeply about what's best for ourselves.

Please understand; the last thing I want to do is blame the victim. I know, love, and regularly counsel survivors. Let me be clear:

---

9 Rhitu Chatterjee, "A New Survey Finds 81 Percent of Women Have Experienced Sexual Harassment," *National Public Radio*, February 21, 2018, https://www.npr.org/.

10 Eberstadt, *Primal*, 96.

any sexual advance, uninvited or unwelcome, is always wrong. But we have to be honest in admitting that the Sexual Revolution set the stage for all kinds of confusion and exploitation on behalf of both men and women. It put us all in a tenuous position. There's no longer the security and safety of fidelity and monogamy, or even a widespread cultural definition of what constitutes good or acceptable behavior.

Relationships are now vague, lines are blurred. Dating apps like Tinder prevail, and consent apps like LegalFling are somehow necessary. Again, sex is pervasive but intimacy is elusive, and we're all the worse for it.

Remember *Fifty Shades of Gray*? I didn't have to personally read it to know that it is an erotic romance novel, wherein romance actually means sexual abuse and domination by the man over the woman. The book and its sequels were everywhere, even amongst women in the church. The fact that the trilogy is a bestseller and became a movie reveals that American women devoured it and encouraged their friends to as well.

But sexual abuse and domination are evil. They are nothing less than an affront to the holy God who made men, women, and children *imago dei*. Sexual violence is violence of the gravest kind. What kind of people are we to exalt it and pay money to revel in it? What's tragic is that *women especially* consume stories like *Fifty Shades of Gray*. Women applauding their own victimization is heartbreaking. It's madness. It's definitive evidence that we live in a world plagued by sexual confusion and brokenness, and very likely evidence of widespread objectification, abuse, and trauma of the girls who became the women who consume this dark content.

We were born into an age that debases our God, his good gifts, and ourselves, his creatures. It's not okay. And I think the cries of #MeToo have only just begun.

Full Circle at the Women's March

Since 2017 millions of women have gathered around the nation each year to participate in the Women's March. The march is a women-led movement "committed to dismantling systems of oppression."[11] According to the march's website, women march because they want more inclusivity, self-determination, dignity, and respect.

The irony, though, is that so much dignity and respect for women was lost in second-wave feminism—right where today's marchers are most at home. While the first wave fostered inclusivity and protection, the second wave fostered objectification and vulnerability. Today's marchers fail to make the connection. In the Sexual Revolution we pursued freedom—throwing off tradition and especially Christian morals. But rather than freedom, we got exploitation and abuse.

Women now march to end the violence our predecessors unknowingly ushered in just decades ago.

Historian Tom Holland says, "Implicit in #MeToo [is] the same call to sexual continence that had reverberated throughout the Church's history."[12] Their cry is for the communal good, for social boundaries and structures that are others-centered, that protect the vulnerable and the marginalized.

---

11 "Mission and Principles," Women's March (website), https://womensmarch.com/mission-and-principles.

12 Tom Holland, *Dominion: How the Christian Revolution Remade the World* (New York: Hachette, 2019), 531.

Whether they know it or not, the cries of Women's March participants are for a *return* to a biblical ethic, a *return* to the Christian conventions and convictions that actually protect women and girls.

But confusion remains. Women's marchers think freedom is found in abortion, in more creative expressions of sexuality, in greater self-focus. The victims of #MeToo think clearer consent laws or more partners will bring them more power. Girls are told everything from "embrace and display your inner twerker" all the way to "throw off the shackles of your gender and come out as a boy instead."

Each iteration of the Sexual Revolution further ensnares, further enslaves, and further exploits women and girls. We're now bearing witness to not just the third wave of feminism, but the fourth. Women are hungry for healing and wholeness, but they continue to put their hope in new counterfeits of a forever-flawed ideology. Maybe one more wave of feminism, maybe one more march, we hope, will get us there.

The truth is, we all—secular and spiritual alike—know there's something terribly wrong with the way women and girls are treated in this lifetime. There's an awareness across the Western world that women and girls have been commodified and used. But it's precisely *because of* "two thousand years of Christian sexual morality [that] men as well as women widely take this for granted."[13]

#MeToo never would have happened without millennia of influence from the Bible.

#MeToo is not just the result of the Sexual Revolution; it is the outworking of an intrinsic awareness of right and wrong, an inherent ethic within us that says we deserve more. This inner

---

13 Holland, *Dominion*, 531.

awareness is our Western heritage, a hidden compass inside our Western DNA, and it harkens us back to those first centuries of Christianity, when women and baby girls were cherished rather than consumed.

Coming to Ourselves in the Far Country

We know something is amiss precisely *because* we in the West have been shaped by Christianity. Human dignity and worth, reverence for both genders, and human rights are not self-evident. They are not venerated truths across all cultures and all time. They are *biblical truths*. And such truths shaped our history and our values whether we acknowledge it or not.

For millennia we in the West said it's good for women and children to enjoy the protections of the law—to be shielded from predators, to require the commitment of marriage, to ensure two-parent homes, and much more. When we threw those boundaries off in the name of freedom, we removed our own protection as well.

But here we are. Like the Prodigal Son, we've come to ourselves out in this far country. The last sixty years of claims to freedom have not been truly freeing. We squandered our Father's good gifts in reckless living. We're hurt and hungry and longing for home. The women in red cloaks and white bonnets are right to cry out and demand better treatment. Like the Prodigal, they hunger for pig's food, when they could be feasting in our Father's house.

And this is why Christianity is predominantly female. In the presence of God and surrounded by his people we are really valued, really loved, and really protected. Oh, that all women in the West would see—*truly see*—the goodness of our God and the goodness of his design for us, his people, *imago dei*.

You and I were made for so much more.

Discussion Questions

1. Have you had a sneaking suspicion that Christianity is bad for women? Share your thoughts with the others in your group.

2. Are you surprised to learn that Christianity is and always has been predominantly female? Discuss the values and cultural practices of the first-century Greco-Roman world, as well as those of the early church.

3. What circumstances brought about first-wave feminism?

4. Have you ever thought about how second-wave feminism in the 1960s defined gender equality as *sameness*? What do you think about how the male body was normed over the female body and preference was given to avoiding or ending pregnancy, rather than anticipating it and celebrating it?

5. The #MeToo movement is not just the result of the Sexual Revolution; it is the outworking of an intrinsic awareness of right and wrong. Everyone—including those who reject Christianity—know women and girls deserve protection precisely *because* we in the West have been shaped by Christianity. How would you help a friend who does not have a biblical worldview connect the dots from her desire for fair treatment to the reality of *imago dei*? What specifically would you say to her?

6. Read Genesis 1:26–28 and 1 Corinthians 6:12–20. Discuss the *imago dei* and the uniqueness of sexual sin. Close by praying and asking God to help you understand both of these themes as they come up throughout the remainder of this book and in everyday life.

3

A Timeless Lens for
Changing Trends

WHEN I WAS A GIRL, my dad tried to talk me out of my Christian faith. I was nine when I heard about Jesus and his love for me. That was when my mom first took me to church, after she and my dad divorced. When I heard the gospel, by God's grace and kindness alone I believed.

I don't blame my dad. When he heard about my plans to make a confession of faith and be baptized in the church, he felt I had been tricked, maybe brainwashed. Now that I'm a parent, I can see how disconcerting it would be for a child of mine to pursue a worldview so in opposition to my own.

My dad was an attorney, and he asked good questions. I had no desire to follow a false faith, and I really wanted to please him. I wanted him to know that I had thought this through, that I wasn't being manipulated by anyone. And so as a teenager I was compelled to look into the veracity of the resurrection, how we got the canon of Scripture, and the historicity of both the Old and New Testaments. If you haven't already, I encourage you to do the same.

Many of us never do this because we live in a culture that rewards distraction, consuming content for pleasure, and binge-watching much more than existential questions. Even when we had extra time on our hands during a global pandemic, how many Americans watched hours and hours of *Tiger King* on Netflix rather than read deeply to get to the bottom of why we believe what we believe? Even as hundreds of thousands died around the world, we numbed our minds rather than sharpened them.

It's easy to do, because we're immersed in soundbites and syncretism. We often—usually unknowingly—invite a conglomeration of conflicting ideas into our hearts and minds. All at once we like to abide by the Golden Rule from Christianity, some Zen from the East, a little karma here, some penance there.

What concerns me about this way of life, though, is that our hodgepodge leaves us wanting.

It's chaos out here in the twenty-first century. We saw in the last chapter how quickly culture can change, how abruptly and absolutely societal convictions and values can be turned upside down. We need a timeless and true lens through which to view ever-changing trends.

That's what this chapter is all about—preparing you and me, growing in us a reality-based understanding of ourselves and our world, so that we are ready for whatever comes. Not only will we be ready for the trials and tribulations that happen to us, but we will also be equipped to sift the chaos that swirls around us.

In this chapter we're going to ask and answer some foundational questions that will build a bedrock for our faith so that we are able to stand, come what may. We'll examine what God is like, what we are like, and what our world is like. This reality-based perspective will enable you and me to identify counterfeits whether they loom far out on the horizon or lurk right here inside us. Remember, human well-being requires harmony with reality. So let's ground ourselves in what's real.

Who Is God?

Our world had a personal beginning, not an impersonal, random one. Our Creator put forth thought and love, and out of his goodness he called the universe, including us, into existence. God's personal love is the foundation for the universe, for everything.[1]

And the world teems with evidence of that love, as well as our Creator's personality, thoughtfulness, and delight: a glittery night sky, a bright red sunset, the shimmering scales on a lizard's back, the enormity of a three-hundred-thousand-pound blue whale, the power of the Zambezi River as it plummets down Victoria Falls, a baby's giggle, a new puppy's breath, the melody of stringed and woodwind instruments playing in unison, sour lemons, and sweet blueberries.

"God is love" (1 John 4:8), says the apostle John, and so says the world around us.

While it's true that God is transcendent—he is above creation, he is the source of it, he is the author and authority of all that we see—it's also true that he's equally imminent. He is personal, active, and involved with his creation. He is not cold and distant, a lifeless statue with arms crossed and impossible to please. He is a personal God who "personally created the world to be populated by people."[2]

God is relational. We can see this first in his own nature, as he is one God in three persons: Father, Son, and Holy Spirit. And we

---

1 Douglas Groothuis, *Christian Apologetics: A Comprehensive Case for Biblical Faith* (Downers Grove, IL: InterVarsity Press, 2011), 84.

2 Groothuis, *Christian Apologetics*, 82.

can see it secondly in how he relates to us. He did not make us because he was lonely but because he is good and loving. He does not stand far off. He is intimately involved in our own stories, as they flow out of his.

This is our God: good, kind, loving, personal, driven to relate to you and me. He has named every star (Ps. 147:4) and, at the same time, he knows just what you and I need before we even ask him (Matt. 6:8).

Who Are We?

You likely already know that God created Adam and Eve on the sixth day of his creating work. During the first five days he made light, the heavens and earth, the sea and the sky, a fertile earth with vegetation, the sun, moon, and stars, and the birds and fish. Then on the sixth day, God brought forth land animals and the first humans, Adam and Eve.

What you may not have considered, though, is how we were made to be cocreators and cocultivators with the Lord, and how we were made for community with one another. As discussed in chapter 2, Genesis 1 says God made man in his own image, *imago dei* (Gen. 1:27). We begin to understand what that means when God blesses Adam and Eve and tells them to be "fruitful and multiply and fill the earth and subdue it and have dominion over the . . . earth" (Gen. 1:28). Part of what it means to be made in God's image is to be a cocreator and a cocultivator with him: to bring forth life and to care for it. We are to nurture what has been made, because behold, it's all very good (Gen. 1:31).

Genesis 2 zooms in on the creation account and tells us three more instructive details about the creation of Adam and Eve. First, we see their creation couched in "the generations of the heavens and the earth" (Gen. 2:4). And twenty-five more times after that the Bible lists one version or another of our genealogy—the generations of us, God's people. Second, Moses tells us that "the LORD God formed the man of dust from the ground and breathed into his nostrils the breath of life, and the man became a living creature" (Gen. 2:7). And third, while Adam slept, God took out one of his ribs and with it made Eve (Gen. 2:21–22). The creation of humans concludes with, "Therefore a man shall leave his father and his mother and hold fast to his wife, and they shall become one flesh. And the man and his wife were both naked and were not ashamed" (Gen. 2:24–25).

The story of humans has always been communal and never individual.

We are a people who come from generations, who come from the dust of the earth and the breath of God. We are never self-made or isolated, and we never have been. We are couched in community, interdependent with others, and dependent on God.

Who we are has everything to do with *whose* we are. We belong to the Lord, our Maker, and we belong to one another.

What Are We Here For?

Have you ever looked deep into your morning coffee and wondered, "What am I even doing here, anyway?" I certainly have. And not just into my coffee. Into textbooks, babies' diapers, moving boxes, social media, the bathroom mirror. It's a good question worth asking.

Our purpose in this life is to reflect our Maker, our God in heaven—we are, after all, *imago dei*. Theologian and author Russell Moore says that "humanity is created to be a sign of God's presence in a unique way."[3] He says we are meant to reveal a longing,

---

3   J. T. English, Jen Wilkin, and Kyle Worley, "Episode #87: Imago Dei and Cultural Mandate with Dr. Russell Moore," October 7, 2020, *Knowing Faith*, podcast, https://podcasts.apple .com/us/podcast/knowing-faith/id1274228164?i=1000493992820.

to give voice to the groaning of creation (Rom. 8:22) that what we see in the material world is not all there is. Our very nature points away from ourselves and cries out *there's something more out there, something more to this life than what you see.* Remember that quiet, second story in our heads that we discussed in chapter 1? This is why that story, that sense of more, persists from the backs of our minds. We were made to think this way.

While we all have the same purpose—to glorify our God—we are a diverse people with innumerable and unique contexts, callings, skills, and burdens. Our God is creative, and he made an immeasurable diversity of people to reflect him. The way you and I create and cultivate will not look the same, but we are each designed to bring order, beauty, and harmony to the place where God has us. That might be in your own home, on Wall Street, in politics, in overseas missions, in your cul-de-sac, or in your city.

Wherever you are, how can you see—*really see*—the people and places around you and bring the good, the beautiful, and the true image of God to bear on that setting? To do so is to bring God glory. It is to create his kingdom on earth, as it is in heaven. We were made for this.

But There's a Problem

Our review so far of who God is, who we are, and what we're supposed to be doing here has been all well and good, except that you likely know we have a problem. Our design has been marred and our roles frustrated.

Let's fill in the rest of the story before we go on. This might feel like a theological detour at the moment, but this is the gospel, the good news for everyone, and we're going to need it fresh on our minds when we get into the next part of the book on idolatry.

Knowing, cherishing, and rehearsing this good news now will prepare us to confront the counterfeits of our age in the coming pages.

Genesis 3 ushers in the fall, or sin, which we looked at briefly in chapter 1. You may recall that the serpent who "was more crafty than any other beast of the field that the LORD God had made" (Gen. 3:1) approached Eve, along with Adam, and questioned God's command that they not eat of the tree of the knowledge of good and evil, lest they die (Gen. 2:17).

Implied is the serpent's suspicion of God's goodness. His goal was to make our first parents suspicious too. He hinted that God was holding out on Adam and Eve, that they would not die, but really live—have their eyes opened and be more like God (Gen. 3:4–5). And so they ate.

That original sin affects us all. The harmony we once enjoyed with our Creator and his world is now broken.

Our One and Only Hope

How many times have you looked into a friend's eyes, brimming with tears, pain etched into the lines on her face, and wanted so badly to have just the right words, the exact answer to what she's going through, an explanation that everything's going to be all right? Living in a post–Genesis 3 world means that scenario is all too common and way too familiar.

After the fall, we are all in need of redemption. And praise God above, we have a Redeemer. As surely as sin entered the world through one man, so did redemption. Begotten of the first Adam, we all experience death and commit sin, but begotten of Jesus—the second and final Adam—we receive grace and everlasting life (Rom. 5:17).

We look ahead with longing and joy and excitement to restoration. Christian, we must remember there is hope on the horizon. Heaven is real. We who trust Jesus *will* rise with him and enjoy him forever. The very reason we can look ahead to "a kingdom that cannot be shaken" (Heb. 12:28) is because of what Jesus has already accomplished for you and me.

Jesus, who is fully God, did not grasp onto all of his privileges as God, but emptied himself, left heaven, and became a man who walked on our broken, post–Genesis 3 earth (Phil. 2:6–7). As fully God and fully man, he is able to sympathize with our weaknesses. He was even tempted as we are, but never sinned (Heb. 4:15). In his time on earth Jesus drew near to broken and suffering people. When he saw us, he had compassion on us, because we "were harassed and helpless, like sheep without a shepherd" (Matt. 9:36). He "went throughout all the cities and villages . . . proclaiming the gospel of the kingdom and healing every disease and every affliction" (Matt. 9:35). While on earth Jesus formed deep relationships and exhibited tender care, weeping even with those who wept (John 11:35).

And here's the great scandal of our faith: while we were still weak, still ungodly, and carrying out our own desires as God's enemies, Christ died for us (Rom. 5:6, 8; Eph. 2:1, 3, 5). Because God is rich in mercy, and because he loves us with a great love (Eph. 2:4), God "made him to be sin who knew no sin, so that in him we might become the righteousness of God" (2 Cor. 5:21).

You and I who trust and follow Jesus are healed—forever and ever healed. My husband frequently reminds me that our biggest problem has already been forever solved. We have been reconciled to our holy, good, Creator God. And now nothing—*nothing*—can "separate us from the love of God in Christ Jesus our Lord" (Rom. 8:39).

When I look into the tear-filled eyes of a friend, or when my own spill over, I look to the cross and I remember. I remember Christ's beaten body, shed blood, great shame, and abandonment on the cross, where he took on the punishment that I deserve.

When I remember the cross, I know I can trust Jesus because of what he has already done for me, the great lengths he has suffered for me. Truly, God is love. He is good. We can trust the God-man who took our sure destruction and gave us everlasting life instead.

Propelled by Freedom

As I shared at the beginning of this chapter, when I was a nine-year-old I confessed, believed, and was saved (Rom. 10:9), but it wasn't until almost a decade later that I really, *experientially knew* the truth, and the truth set me free (John 8:32). As the reality of the great exchange—my sin for Jesus's perfection—sank into my soul, I was freed from the pressure to perform for the acceptance and love of God and others. I was freed from sin that had ensnared, freed from both pride and self-loathing, freed from fear of my future and what may or may not happen to me, freed from the fear of death and sickness and pain.

Of course these false masters still crouch and prowl in wait (Gen. 4:7; 1 Pet. 5:8), and they will until I reach heaven, but they no longer enslave me. They no longer get the ultimate say. The truth has set me free.

This freedom in Christ is the *so much more* we were made for. This is our eternal, already-sealed, unshakable hope: "We are not our own but belong, body and soul, both in life and death, to God and to our Savior Jesus Christ."[4] You and I who follow Jesus have

---

4   *The New City Catechism: 52 Questions and Answers for Our Hearts and Minds* (Wheaton, IL, Crossway, 2017), 17.

been "delivered from the domain of darkness and transferred to the kingdom of the beloved Son" (Col. 1:13). It is settled. We are secure, safe, and lavishly loved.

All that we need, we have in Christ Jesus our Lord. And that can never, ever be snatched away (John 10:28). We are free, truly free! This changes everything.

If you are a Christian, then you have so much more in Christ than this world is able to offer you. Because we have abundant life in Jesus (John 10:10), because we have every spiritual blessing from our good God (Eph. 1:3), because we are dearly loved adopted children with an inheritance from the Creator of the universe (Eph. 1:5, 11), we can seek first his kingdom (Matt. 6:33), we can pursue God's will on earth as it is in heaven (Matt. 6:10). We have this so-much-more treasure in jars of clay (2 Cor. 4:7), and we are called to share it with others.

We are Christ's ambassadors (2 Cor. 5:20), and he asks us to proclaim what's true, real, and freeing to all people, to all the nations (Matt. 28:19–20). This is our joy and this is our mission: to walk in the fullness of life and deep-down gladness that's available in Christ alone and to share that with others.

From Fake to Facts

In the next part of the book we're going to take a deep dive into five empty promises of our age that have been especially attractive, deceptive, and deadly (physically and spiritually) to women. We have settled for so little. We have bowed down at the altars of outward beauty and ability, cheap sex, abortion, gender and sexual fluidity, and even marriage and motherhood. We've sought our value, identity, and real joy in cheap fakes rather than the real thing.

So many of us don't even know we're bowing down to false gods, which are being passed off as the real deal. Like "Rolexes" on Canal

Street in New York City, we glance at them but don't scrutinize them. They look pretty good, we think, nothing better to compare them to. We pay the cheap price, put them on, and rely on them to direct our day.

Really, we have just been far too easily pleased. We've settled for the knockoff version of life and femaleness because we didn't know there was something better. The voices of the vendors hawking their false wares have drowned out the better voices. We haven't even heard the best voice—God's voice.

I'm moved to write because I've been there. And this side of heaven, I'm still there in ways that I don't perceive even now, and some that I do. In so many ways I have been duped, wearing "Rolexes" all the way up both forearms. My life has been littered with counterfeits because I either didn't know better or because I lacked the faith to believe that God's ways really are for my good, and your good, and *everyone's* good.

Now that I have seen these counterfeits under the light, I'm looking at my arms and thinking, *These dumb watches aren't even real.* They've been weighing me down, sucking the life out of me. And this whole time I thought they looked good, empowering even, signs to the world that I am a capable, thoughtful, and modern woman.

My hope is that in the light of beautiful truth and with God's help, you and I will remove one counterfeit at a time and replace each one with the truly magnificent real deal. You and I and every woman and girl who has ever lived is a creature with a Creator. We have a glorious design because we have a glorious Designer.

How Then Should We Live?

My dad was worried about my young faith because he knew, rightly received and rightly applied, it would change everything. He knew our worldviews would diverge and we would see everything from politics to business to art to economics differently. He was right. Christ-carriers in the midst of our fallen world will not follow the status quo. We must live in accordance with reality, in agreement with what's true.

What's true is that human well-being requires harmony with reality. And reality is found in the pages of the word of God; indeed, God himself is ultimate reality. Knowing he is our Creator and we are his creatures leads us to live in light of two truths.

First, we belong to God. Every human being owes his or her existence to the God who made us. It's his breath in our lungs. It is he who created us in our mother's wombs (Ps. 139:15). And this truth is even more powerful for those who profess Christ. As the apostle Jude says, Christ is "our only Master and Lord" (Jude 4). The Holy Spirit himself dwells in us; we are temples of the one true God. You and I were bought at the price of Jesus Christ crucified. It is our call and honor to glorify him with our bodies (1 Cor. 6:19–20).

Second, we belong to each other. None of us are self-made or self-sufficient. Every genealogy in the Bible reminds us that all humans—whether we each believe God's word or not—are interrelated and interdependent. We need each other, and we are called to love one another, "for the whole law is fulfilled in one word: 'You shall love your neighbor as yourself'" (Gal. 5:14). Loving one another, though, is rarely automatic or easy. We have to lay ourselves down, as Jesus did. And loving in a distinctly Christian way will surely go against the cultural grain.

We in the West have largely accepted and embraced the counterfeits of our day. And though they've promised life, they've delivered death. The truth about who God is, who we are, and how he designed us to live is our only hope.

As we uncover the counterfeits of our age and recover timeless truths for every age, may the truth set us free.

Discussion Questions

1. When you look at creation, what's your favorite thing to behold? What does it tell you about the personal love of God?

2. Read Genesis 2 all the way through. What do you think about the truth that we are never self-made or isolated, and never have been? How hard is it to live in the twenty-first century according to the truth that we are meant to be couched in community, interdependent with others, and dependent on God?

3. The *New City Catechism* says, "This present fallen world is not all there is; soon we will enjoy God forever in the new city, in the new heaven and the new earth, where we will be fully and forever freed from all sin and will inhabit renewed, resurrection bodies in a renewed, restored creation."[5] How does this truth about the future affect how you live in the present? Or, if it doesn't affect how you currently live, what might you change in light of it?

4. Read Romans 5:6–8, 2 Corinthians 5:21, and Ephesians 2:1–10. How do these truths help you trust Jesus right now?

5. Jesus says if we are his disciples, then we will know the truth and the truth will set us free (John 8:32). Can you think of a time when you believed a lie—when you wore a fake Rolex, to use my example from the chapter—and then became aware that it was a fake?

5 *New City Catechism*, question 52.

6. Share with each other what you think is meant by the phrase "human well-being requires harmony with reality." This truism will come up a lot in the chapters ahead. Close by praying and asking God to help you see and believe what is true and that the truth will indeed set you free.

PART 2

CONFRONTING THE EMPTY PROMISES OF OUR AGE

Idols and their empty promises are as old as we humans are. But in the twenty-first century West there are at least five that have proven to be especially winsome and tragically destructive to women and girls. Part 2 seeks to uncover those idols and expose them for the counterfeits they really are.

> Come, everyone who thirsts,
>   come to the waters;
> and he who has no money,
>   come, buy and eat!
> Come, buy wine and milk
>   without money and without price.
> Why do you spend your money for that which is not bread,

and your labor for that which does not satisfy?
Listen diligently to me, and eat what is good,
    and delight yourselves in rich food.
Incline your ear, and come to me;
    hear, that your soul may live. (Isa. 55:1–3)

4

Obsessed: Bodies, Beauty, and Ability

"MOMMY, DO I LOOK PRETTY?" As a mom of four daughters I heard that question every day for years. We had bins full of princess dresses and costumes. The more glitter and bling the better. Evidently two, or even three, princess dresses layered on top of one another really are better than just one.

They're teens and young adults now, evolving more into my girlfriends and confidants with each passing year. Now they ask, "Does this look okay?" And I frequently ask them the same question in return. I think we're pretty low maintenance, but my husband marvels at how many outfits we Oshwomen might try on before exiting the house.

The first time my first daughter asked if I thought she looked pretty, my heart raced as I tried to formulate an answer. It's a loaded question, even if the asker is unaware. On one hand, I wanted to blurt out, "Of course you do! You are gorgeous!" I certainly thought all of my little girls were beautiful, and I delighted to see them don whatever fancied their imaginations.

On the other hand, from the moment I heard "It's a girl!" in the ultrasound room, I wanted so badly to protect my daughters from an unhealthy, idolatrous view of their bodies. I didn't want them to fall into the pervasive Western way of placing their value in how they looked or what they could do. I wanted my girls to follow Jesus and know that appearance and ability are not of ultimate importance.

How do you help a three-year-old understand that, yes indeed, you do think she is the most beautiful girl you've ever seen, but also make her know deep down in her soul that our beauty is intrinsic simply because we're human beings? How do you teach a toddler that beauty is far, far more than tiaras and lace? How do you help a thirteen-year-old understand that? A thirty-year-old? A seventy-five-year-old?

My mom cracked up years ago when I reminded her how she responded to me when I asked her if I looked pretty as a little girl. Her repeated response, which she now promises she cannot remember, was, "Don't put too much hope in how pretty you are. You could be in a car accident today that would disfigure your face forever, and then what would you do?" We had a good howl over her bluntness back then (which is a window into what it was like to be raised in the 1980s), but I assure you it haunted me for years. *What if an accident like that happened? Do I care too much about my physical appearance and abilities?*

The truth is, perfect appearances and perfectly able bodies are ethereal, the stuff of imaginations and computer-generated imagery (CGI). And yet, we who inhabit the real world are nonetheless fixated on them.

What is the right way to live in a culture that is obsessed with our bodies?

Beautiful People

It's the beautiful people amongst us who take center stage. Movie stars, news anchors, and almost every public persona are adorned with beautiful faces. We prioritize the pretty ones, putting them on pedestals, and relegate the average and "ugly" faces to behind the scenes and behind the cameras.

Economists and sociologists have even proven how financially helpful it is to be good-looking. Daniel Hamermesh, an economics professor and author of *Beauty Pays*, says, "One study showed that an American worker who was among the bottom one-seventh in looks, as assessed by randomly chosen observers, earned 10 to 15 percent less per year than a similar worker whose looks were assessed in the top one-third."[1] That is a lifetime difference in earnings of about $270,000 in today's economy.

Hamermesh says it's a matter of prejudice. We gravitate toward attractive salespeople, clients and customers, attorneys, teachers, coaches, politicians, and everyone else. We all contribute to a cycle that rewards a certain aesthetic.

Knowing that beauty is advantageous, we spend ample time and money on improving our good looks. The United States is "home to the largest beauty and personal care market in the world. In 2019, it was valued at about 93.35 billion U.S. dollars, up from 80.7 billion dollars in 2015."[2]

Business Insider says growth in the beauty industry has really taken off in the past few years because of social media. "Cosmetic

---

1 Daniel S. Hamermesh, "Ugly? You May Have a Case," *New York Times* online, August 27, 2011, https://www.nytimes.com/.

2 Alexander Kunst, "Average Amount Consumers Spend on Beauty and Personal Care Products Per Month in the United States as of May 2017," Statista (website), December 20, 2019, https://www.statista.com/statistics/715231/average-monthly-spend-on-beauty-products-us/.

companies [are] tapping into the power of influencer marketing and brand ambassadors."[3] We see beautiful faces on social media—often our friends or friends of friends—and we want whatever product they're peddling.

Reels Aren't Real

My husband and I are sticks-in-the-mud when it comes to our daughters and social media. We don't have any hard-and-fast rules, and we don't want to forbid it forever, but we do want to delay the soul-deadening effects for as long as possible. We know their teen hearts are tender, and we want them to grow and thrive without that pressure for as long as we can all hold out. I'm in my forties, and I struggle with followers and likes and wanting to pose just right to avoid a double chin. How much more would that have ensnared my sixteen- or thirteen-year-old self?

Author and smartphone critic Tony Reinke says, "In the age of spectacle, image is our identity, and our identity is unavoidably molded by our media."[4] Not only is our identity now self-constructed, as we looked at in chapter 2, but we *construct it online* where we have an endless option of filters and photo editing apps. We craft our image digitally, championing the *appearance of who we are* above and beyond who we really, truly are.

What I'm actually like in real life matters less than how I project that image online.

These small, sinister social media squares are discipling us. They are shaping the way you and I and our daughters (and sons) think

3   Bethany Biron, "Beauty Has Blown Up to Be a $532 Billion Industry—and Analysts Say That These 4 Trends Will Make It Even Bigger," *Business Insider* online, July 9, 2019, https://www.businessinsider.com.

4   Tony Reinke, *Competing Spectacles: Treasuring Christ in the Media Age* (Wheaton, IL: Crossway, 2019), 21.

about ourselves, our identity, and our worth. Like a slow drip that shapes a deep canyon, the consumption for hours a day of media held in our hands is carving how we see humans, the meaning and value of life, and what ultimately matters. We don't have to be conscious of it to be greatly affected by it.

You and I and the 75 percent of the American population who use social media every day are ingesting everyone else's highlight reels and internalizing those images *as real*.[5] From famous to obscure, every avatar displays his or her best moments. Months and years of ingesting digitally enhanced and manufactured squares is changing you and me.

Hustle Culture

Consistently shaped by so many visuals of the good life, we set out to fabricate our best lives too. We answer emails at all hours hoping to close the deal and striving to grow a following to expand our influence. We hustle so we can have it all.

Hustle culture spills over into our nonwork lives too, making them feel oddly like work. We toil at the gym and count our carbs to get that beach body; we pursue the perfect plans (weekend, college, retirement, and vacation); we curate our best wardrobes, the right hair color, the perfect wine and cheese pairing, and the nontoxic friend group who will help us get to where we want to go. Hustle culture is born out of that first story we looked at in chapter 1—it's the story in your head that says *you can be awesome, you just have to make it happen.*

Smartphones serve as ever-present curators to photograph and display each on-brand scene. One square at a time, we become products

5   "Social Media Fact Sheet," Pew Research Center, June 12, 2019, https://www.pewresearch.org/.

for others to consume. Professor and culture writer Anne Helen Peterson says young adults "are far less jealous of objects or belongings on social media than the holistic experiences represented there, the sort of thing that prompts people to comment, *I want your life.* That enviable mix of leisure and travel, the accumulation of pets and children, the landscapes inhabited and the food consumed seems not just desirable, but balanced, satisfied, and unafflicted by burnout."[6]

We're adept at posting the good life even when we don't feel it or actually live it.

How many times a day do you and I curate our lives and lifestyles? And how many times a day does our blood pressure rise just a bit as we sense that it's not enough? So we keep hustling, keep hoping, keep aiming for that perfect image—or at least the *appearance* of the perfect image.

Throwaway Culture

As we hustle to grab hold of the good life and to curate and broadcast our best images, slow, intentional living is left behind. Hustling requires disposing more than sustaining. Branding can't be bothered with what appears less than perfect. In pursuit of the highlight reel, anything troublesome must be tossed.

"Throwaway Living" was first documented in a 1955 *Life* magazine article that celebrated the advent of disposable items, which cut down on household chores.[7] Everything from paper plates to disposable diapers to throwaway draperies to a "disposa-pan" are commended because they don't need to be washed or cared for—

6 Anne Helen Petersen, "How Millennials Became the Burnout Generation," *Buzzfeed News*, January 5, 2019, https://www.buzzfeednews.com/.

7 "Throwaway Living," *Life*, August 1, 1955, 43–44, Google Books, https://books.google.ca.

just tossed into the trash can. Since then, the term "throwaway society" has been used as a label for our habits of consuming and creating waste.

We know from the historical context of chapter 2 that 1955 was right before the Sexual Revolution exploded. Urbanization and technologization had been affecting American households for decades. Communal living decreased, while autonomy increased. Disposable plates are now just an emblem of the convenience Westerners have come to expect since the middle of last century.

Fast forward almost seventy years, and we cannot imagine living without so many more modern conveniences, because our pace and pursuits demand it. With the ubiquity of smartphones and Wi-Fi we're connected like never before, but lonelier than ever. Our online relationships can go only so deep, and hustle culture doesn't have much time for real people in real life.

Throwaway culture may now be applied well beyond paper products. Tragically, it can be said of the way we treat people too.

From Appearance to Ability to Abortion

On the social media reel the realities of sickness and enduring through suffering are rarely featured. Our obsession with our bodies goes well beyond how we appear to what we can *do*. When our bodies cannot do what we want them to, we deem them (maybe silently and only to ourselves) worth less than bodies that are not hindered or slowed down by age, ailments, or disabilities.

Our focus on what we can do surfaces when we introduce ourselves to new people. It's how we sort each other out when we first meet at church or a dinner party. *What do you do?* we want to know. We see it in other relatively harmless ways too: frustration with getting sick, fighting the need for eight hours of sleep a night, irritation when our to-do lists are not completed. We want to be strong and unstoppable.

What we *do* gives us so much satisfaction that it easily becomes an idol. But our obsession with ability can turn real dark, real quick. A subconscious devotion to beautiful, normalized, fully-able bodies primes you and me to be willing to snuff out anything—*anyone*—less.

Nothing captures this cultural reality better than a 2017 announcement: "Iceland is on pace to virtually eliminate Down syndrome through abortion."[8] While the headline caused rejoicing amongst many, it isn't true. Iceland is not eliminating Down syndrome; it's eliminating babies. Down syndrome is viewed as less than beautiful, less than able, less than desirable, and Iceland is leading the way in targeting and killing babies in the womb who are given a high probability of having this specific genetic difference. Throughout Europe and North America such testing and eliminating are now commonplace.

Doctors use ultrasounds, blood tests, and the mother's age to compute the probability for a baby to be born with the syndrome. Parents decide after hearing a number—something like, *Your baby will have a one in one hundred chance of having Down syndrome*—whether or not to terminate the pregnancy. In Iceland nearly 100 percent of parents terminate, in Denmark it's 98 percent, in France it's 77 percent, and in the United States it's 67 percent.[9]

In 2019 in Denmark just eighteen babies were born with Down syndrome, eleven of those were false negatives, and only seven were couples who decided to carry and deliver their babies with a relatively

8 CBSNews (@CBSNews), Twitter, August 14, 2017, 6:30 p.m., https://twitter.com/CBSNews/status/897254042178650113.
9 Julian Quinones and Arijeta Lajka, "'What Kind of Society Do You Want to Live In?': Inside the Country Where Down Syndrome Is Disappearing," *CBS News*, August 14, 2017, https://www.cbsnews.com/.

high chance of having Down syndrome. One Danish mother who delivered after a false negative admitted, "We would have asked for an abortion if we knew."[10] She voices the often hushed, but nevertheless real, feelings of a growing number of parents of children born with disabilities. Lawsuits are popping up all over the United States wherein mothers sue sperm banks and sperm donors for characteristics they deem undesirable, which appear only after birth.

The options for genetic selection expand every year, as technology improves. Preimplantation Genetic Testing (PGT) is available to parents who use in vitro fertilization (IVF). After sperm and egg are united to form an embryo, geneticists can test for the presence of genes carrying everything from cystic fibrosis to intellectual disabilities before implantation. "The one test customers keep asking for," according to a testing firm in New Jersey, "is for autism. The science isn't there yet, but the demand is."[11]

Humans now have the power to determine what kind of lives should be brought into the world and which ones should be destroyed beforehand. We've already seen this in India and China, which together account for the vast majority of the estimated 1.2 million to 1.5 million missing female births annually worldwide due to pre-birth sex selection.[12] Additionally, the ability to edit the genes of an embryo, using new CRISPR technology, is moving faster than agreed-upon ethics around the globe.[13]

---

10 Sarah Zhang, "The Last Children of Down Syndrome," *The Atlantic*, December 2020, https://www.theatlantic.com/.

11 Zhang, "The Last Children."

12 "India Accounts for 45.8 Million of the World's 'Missing Females': UN report," *The Economic Times*, June 30, 2020, https://economictimes.indiatimes.com.

13 For more see John Stonestreet, "The Point: Altering Our DNA for Good?," *Breakpoint*, August 1, 2019, https://www.breakpoint.org/.

Babies are already products and parents are already shoppers who can browse and spend and throw away in pursuit of just the right physical and mental traits they're looking for.

From Appearance to Ability to Assisted Suicide

This kind of godlike decision-making is increasing on the other end of the life spectrum too. Assisted suicide gained national notoriety in 2014 when Brittany Maynard, a twenty-nine-year-old with brain cancer and a terminal diagnosis, moved from California to Oregon to end her life under that state's "Death with Dignity Act." Her raw social media posts highlighted her young and vibrant life taking a nightmarish turn with the diagnosis and subsequent seizures, head and neck pain, and stroke-like symptoms. On November 1, 2014, she posted the following on social media just prior to ingesting a fatal dose of barbiturates: "Today is the day I have chosen to pass away with dignity in the face of my terminal illness, this terrible brain cancer that has taken so much from me . . . but would have taken so much more."[14]

We see our strong cultural value in Brittany's words: sickness and suffering are a *taking away*, rather than a *contributing to*. To be sick, to be less than fully able, to face a future of increasing pain and disability is something we dislike and reject and want to do away with before we even consider what we're really getting rid of.

Physician-assisted suicide is now legal in nine states plus the District of Columbia. In most cases, patients must have a terminal illness and a prognosis of six months or less to live, and then their doctors can legally prescribe medications to bring about their deaths. In my own state of Colorado, assisted suicide was legalized

---

14 Lindsey Bever, "Brittany Maynard, as Promised, Ends Her Life at 29," *The Washington Post*, November 2, 2014, https://www.washingtonpost.com/.

in 2016; in 2019, 170 prescriptions were written for aid-in-dying medication, and 129 of them were filled.[15]

Opponents of physician-assisted suicide find numerous reasons to oppose this growing trend. Here are just four worth considering:

- Assisted suicide robs patients of compassionate care.
- The right to die leads to a duty to die.
- Assisted suicide ruins trust with doctors.
- Sometimes a terminal diagnosis is wrong.[16]

Volumes could be written on these four reasons alone, but the bottom line is that "death with dignity" is really death without, or at least too little, dignity. "Death with dignity" disposes of life far too quickly. Death with genuine dignity would include a team of compassionate professionals and loved ones embracing the sufferer and looking for creative ways to ease his or her pain. The team would do the hard work of drawing near, standing watch, and abiding with the sick to comfort, listen, and soothe them to their natural, God-given end. Despair is a tragedy, and it is also sin. Who are we to encourage despair by saying, "Yes, end it all; your life isn't worth living," when we know God can bring beauty from ashes (Isa. 61:1–3)?

One tragic irony in the speed with which abortion and assisted suicide surge forward is that the medical community and the public at large are now more accepting, compassionate, and equipped to help people with sickness and disabilities navigate a higher quality

---

15 CNN Editorial Research, "Physician-Assisted Suicide Fast Facts," *CNN*, June 11, 2020, https://www.cnn.com.

16 Brooke B. McIntire, "Is Assisted Suicide Really Compassionate?," *Breakpoint*, July 23, 2020, https://www.breakpoint.org/.

of life for a much longer time. But with all of this philosophical and medical progress within our grasp, we are ready to throw it all away, without even using it. With fewer and fewer surviving with a condition (from Down syndrome to end-stage terminal illness), that quality of care will drop off.

Bodies as Instruments

When my girls were born, it felt like a miracle. The doctors laid their tiny frames on my chest, and they opened their blurry eyes and blinked into mine. Delivering them into the world was sacred, and everyone in that room—even the most tenured doctors and nurses—could feel it. There was joy and elation and tears. I don't think anyone ever really gets over the wonder of a new, irreplaceable, unrepeatable life.

How crass, then, to turn a wondrous body into a mere instrument, "treating it as a tool to be used and controlled instead of valuing it for its own sake."[17] This instrumentalization has been hastened and bolstered by our image-driven age. We behold and create images of beauty and ability over and over and dispose of anything less. The images numb us to the reality around us. On a subconscious level we daily, even hourly, reinforce the idea that beautiful and able lives are the best lives.

And Christians, who know we all bear the image of God, are not unscathed. Tony Reinke points us back to the early church theologian and philosopher Augustine, who concluded that the images we consume are, as Reinke writes, "not harmless fun but iceboxes that chill Christian hearts by conditioning viewers to become passive gazers at the troubled plights and needs of the hurting on stage."[18]

---

17 Nancy Pearcey, *Love Thy Body* (Grand Rapids, MI: Baker, 2018), 32.
18 Reinke, *Competing Spectacles*, 71–72.

Christian, has your heart been chilled? Are you a passive gazer of troubled plights? What kind of life do you seek? What kind of life do you protect?

Embodied Souls

A reaction to the objectification of bodies can turn into a back-lash against bodies themselves. *This is just a shell I'm going to leave behind one day*, we think. But bodies are good, and we are infinitely more than instruments. When my pastor-husband stands in front of our church at the end of each service on Sundays to give the benediction, he invites the congregation to stand and says, "Recognizing we are embodied souls, would you put out your hands to receive the benediction?" It's a small gesture, but it's a weekly reminder that what happens to the body, happens to the soul. We are whole humans—both body and soul are present and precious.

When God breathed life into the nostrils of Adam, the first man became alive not just physically but mentally and spiritually too. We "humans are integrated beings . . . embodied and highly developed souls."[19] The Bible teaches that the human body and soul are inseparable.

We see God's enduring value of human bodies from the very beginning. He made man in his image, but in a human body. The plan all along was that God would dwell with us, in human form, in the person of Jesus. Jesus put on flesh and came, in Mary's womb, as a baby to be born in a lowly manger. Immanuel, God with us, God in the flesh. Jesus's resurrection too is an affirmation of the body. His resurrection is a forerunner to ours. The climax

---

19 Douglas Groothuis, *Christian Apologetics: A Comprehensive Case for Biblical Faith* (Downers Grove, IL: InterVarsity Press, 2011), 86.

of God's story in Revelation 21 and 22 tells us that all of God's people, in resurrected bodies, will dwell with him and he with them for eternity.

The Bible has a high view of human bodies and souls, integrated together, revealing God's image to a watching world. Every human body is invaluable because each one bears a soul, each one is *imago dei*, each one was created very good.

Neither Animal nor Divine

As we've said before, human well-being requires harmony with reality. As we walk in the truth about our bodies, we must avoid two common pitfalls found in secular thinking. We are neither inconsequential evolved animals nor supernatural beings ourselves. We are children of God, couched in creation.[20]

In the first pitfall we view our bodies as clumps of cells to be done away with when necessary. We mutated here by chance, this view says, so our highest good is to feel pleasure. Therefore, if we feel pain, it's okay to end it all. In the second pitfall, we balk at our limitations and finiteness and we seek to be our own gods, to create our own selves, to forge our own destinies.

We are neither evolved animals nor divine beings. We are embodied souls formed by a grand and omnipotent God. Two psalms of King David shed light on this crucial truth. He says of God, "You formed my inward parts; / you knitted me together in my mother's womb" (Ps. 139:13). And marveling at all of creation he says, "What is man that you are mindful of him . . . ? Yet you have made him a little lower than the heavenly beings / and crowned him with glory and honor. / You have given him dominion over

---

20 Groothuis, *Christian Apologetics*, 389.

the works of your hands" (Ps. 8:4–6). Not divine, but not mere animals either.

Our bodies are gifts designed by a good, sovereign, beauty-making God. We must care for, protect, and cherish each and every human body, each and every human life. Our conviction as children of God is that these lives are not our own, but belong—body and soul—to the Creator. Life is a gift to steward, not manipulate, exploit, or dispose of as the world sees fit.

Shifting Hope

As a culture we are out in a far country, obsessing over our bodies and counting on them to deliver us power and satisfaction through beauty and ability. But, going back to my mom's point to me when I was a young girl, these bodies are not a guarantee. They can be lost. In fact, living in a post–Genesis 3 world means they will definitely be lost, if not in a sudden calamity, then over time. We must come to ourselves, like the Prodigal Son, and admit that we have sinned against heaven and before God (Luke 15:17–18).

The apostle Paul says outwardly we are wasting away, but there's hope because "our inner self is being renewed day by day" (2 Cor. 4:16). Daily we experience the painful reality that our current bodies languish on the outside, but we have hope because our eternal God renews us on the inside.

Our bodies cannot bear up under the weight of what worldly values want them to deliver. If we're looking to them for meaning, significance, and security, we will be disappointed and even devastated. We were not made to fix our eyes on ourselves or on each other, whether in real life or online. We were made to fix our eyes on Jesus, the author and perfector of our faith (Heb. 12:2). *Hope in God*, as the psalmist says (Ps. 42:5, 11).

The Heart of Beauty

So then, what might it practically look like to place our hope in God and not in our own appearance and abilities? How might we actually apply this in real life? Outward beauty is tricky because it's something we come back to every time we glance in the bathroom mirror. It's something that feels worth at least some time and effort and money. But then just as quickly it feels wrong and ungodly, or like a waste. It's hard to know exactly what Christ-followers ought to pursue here.

As is always the case in the Christian walk, it's the heart that matters. The Lord said to the prophet Samuel, "The LORD sees not as man sees: man looks on the outward appearance, but the LORD looks on the heart" (1 Sam. 16:7). From the heart flows life (Prov. 4:23).

God himself is beautiful, and he is the very maker of beauty. The mountains and seas and colors of creation are breathtakingly beautiful. God is not opposed to outward beauty—he makes it! And we, created in the image of God, love to behold beauty too. We *ooh* and *aah* and experience rejuvenation in beautiful contexts. Therefore, the pursuit of outward beauty is not wrong or sinful when it's grounded in the right heart.

The apostle Peter gives specific instructions here when he says, "Do not let your adorning be external—the braiding of hair and the putting on of gold jewelry, or the clothing you wear—but let your adorning be the hidden person of the heart with the imperishable beauty of a gentle and quiet spirit, which in God's sight is very precious" (1 Pet. 3:3–4). Peter warns us not to put our hope in our hair or jewels or clothing—things that pass away, things that communicate worldly status. Rather, let us hope in what is imperishable, that which is not of this world. May we have hearts centered on the God who does not pass away. May we be gentle and quiet—not fretting, not freaking out—because we trust in Christ Jesus above all else. While we are certainly free to enjoy it, you and I must not depend on outward adornment, because we already have an immovable and inward identity in Christ alone.

Paul tells Timothy that women ought to adorn themselves with "what is proper for women who profess godliness" (1 Tim. 2:10). The questions the Christian woman must consider are, Does my outward appearance profess godliness? Does it reflect my inner heart? Does my hope in God shine through?

May we be so secure in Jesus, so grateful that we have been transferred from the domain of darkness to the kingdom of the beloved Son (Col. 1:13), that it shows. May our emphasis on our outward appearance stay in its rightful place—not the object of our hope, but an expression of the unique, innately beautiful creatures we already are. May we be freed from the world's standard of beauty and commit ourselves to God's standard of beauty. Sure, wear the makeup and jewelry and cute clothes. But don't let them quiet Christ in you, the hope of glory (Col. 1:27). May your outward appearance and mine reveal that we rest and rejoice in a risen Savior and no longer rush to rely on ourselves.

Who Is Able?

Just as the pursuit of beauty is not wrong when it's properly grounded in hope in God, neither is it wrong to pursue one's abilities. In fact, it's wrong *not* to. We are made by God and for God (Col. 1:16). We are called to use our bodies for his glory (1 Cor. 6:20).

When I drive my daughters to school in the morning, we pray on the way. Each day's prayer shares a similar thread. I constantly ask the Lord to help them and to show them how to steward their day, their skills, and their resources for his glory alone. I thank him that their identity is not contingent on making the team or the play or the grade, because their identity is already forever secure in the person and work of Jesus. Even if my prayers sound like a broken record, I think it's worth repeating, as I know they will hear the exact opposite all day long. Their teachers, coaches, and friends will communicate directly or indirectly that their worth is in what they can do. And that's just not true.

Greatness in God's kingdom is the very opposite of greatness in ours. Jesus surprisingly, even scandalously, said, "'Let the children come to me; do not hinder them, for to such belongs the kingdom of God. Truly, I say to you, whoever does not receive the kingdom of God like a child shall not enter it.' And he took them in his arms and blessed them" (Mark 10:14–16). Jesus even said, "Whoever humbles himself like this child is the greatest in the kingdom of heaven" (Matt. 18:4).

The world tells us to trust in ourselves, to try our hardest, to put our hope in our own abilities. But as we approach God, Jesus says we must be like children: weak, vulnerable, and trusting.

In God's view, the last shall be first (Matt. 20:16). The poor in spirit are blessed and the meek inherit the earth (see the Beatitudes in Matt. 5:1–12). We are called to boast in our weaknesses alone, because God's grace is sufficient and his power is made perfect in our weakness (2 Cor. 12:9). As Paul says, we can be "content with weaknesses, insults, hardships, persecutions, and calamities. For when [we are] weak, then [we are] strong" (2 Cor. 12:10).

She who is truly able trusts in Christ alone.

The Truly Beautiful and Productive Life

Everyone—not just little girls—asks, "Do I look pretty?" We all want to know if we are seen, valued, and appreciated. The world's answer to that question, though, is rooted in standards that are far too low, far too temporary, far too shakable.

The body is good and made by God. Beauty and abilities are gifts. But these things are not ultimate. They are given to us to steward, that we may know God and make him known.

It's hard to think of a woman who does this better than well-known author, speaker, and advocate Joni Eareckson Tada. Joni became a quadriplegic over fifty years ago as the result of a tragic diving accident when she was just seventeen. She often repeats the wisdom a friend shared with her decades ago: "God permits what he hates to accomplish what he loves. . . . God hates spinal cord injury, yet he permitted it for the sake of Christ in you—as well as in others."[21]

The world makes empty promises through outward beauty and ability. But you and I were made for so much more. The truly beautiful, truly productive life is the one that carries Christ and puts his goodness on display. And that so often flows from suffering, from trials and persecution, from rejection and sickness. Joni says, "The process is difficult, but affliction isn't a killjoy; I don't think you could find a happier follower of Jesus than me. . . . God shares his joy on his terms only, and those terms call for us to suffer, in some measure, like his Son. I'll gladly take it."[22]

May we all gladly take the life, the body, the beauty, and the abilities that God gives—for our good and his glory.

---

21 Joni Eareckson Tada, "Reflections on the 50th Anniversary of My Diving Accident," The Gospel Coalition, July 30, 2017, https://www.thegospelcoalition.org/.

22 Eareckson Tada, "Reflections."

Discussion Questions

1. What's your childhood history with outward beauty and ability? For example, were you shaped by a certain event or family value, or do you have a story like mine when my mom said, "Don't put too much hope in how pretty you are. You could be in a car accident today that would disfigure your face forever, and then what would you do?"

2. In what ways do you think social media is discipling you?

3. Do you know anyone with Down syndrome or anyone who has a child with it? What do you think of our world's increasing drive to eliminate babies with disabilities? What do you think about physician-assisted suicide? Where do these issues come up in your own life, and how might you be an advocate for life instead of death in your own community?

4. Have you ever thought bodies are just a shell and not really important? What do you think about the truth that we are embodied souls?

5. Is it possible to pursue outward beauty and ability in a way that honors God? What does that look like? What are some truly practical steps you can take to do that more consistently in your own life?

6. Read the Beatitudes in the Sermon on the Mount in Matthew 5:1–12 and reflect on how God's ways are so often different from the world's ways. Read also Matthew 5:13–16, and discuss how you might be "salt and light" and a "city on a hill" in your context. Close by praying and asking God to renew your mind in the areas of outward beauty and ability.

5

Selling Out for Cheap Sex

MARK AND I GOT MARRIED right around the same time *The Bachelor* and *The Bachelorette* debuted. Unless you live under a rock, you know what these "reality" shows are all about. A single guy or gal gluts him or herself on multiple romantic options, multiple sexual encounters, multiple exotic and erotic scenarios, and then picks one spouse from a pool of twenty-five on the season's final episode.

The shows have been called America's favorite guilty pleasure. Even if they seem crazy or conjured up or just totally carnal, people love to tune in. Viewers likely think, *I would never do that*, while thrilling at watching strangers on the screen give it a try. Both shows have been highly rated for two decades and counting.

The Bachelor and *The Bachelorette* tap into our cultural narrative that says playing the field, dating around, and imbibing in myriad sexual options is how you discover yourself. That was definitely the cultural consensus when Mark and I got engaged and married. We were the first amongst our friends to walk the aisle, and we both come from long lines of divorce. Monogamy seemed risky or downright foolish to most of the people in our sphere. I admit that I had to battle this view myself. Our first year of dating was a mess because I had a hard time getting over the idea that to find myself, I needed to date a lot more guys on my college campus. Everyone said that's how you grow up, how you become the woman you're meant to be. It was hard to disagree with parents, coaches, teachers, mentors, and friends who all said the same thing.

Our culture's worship of sex hardly needs to be extrapolated here. You already know it's everywhere. Like a neon sign on the Vegas strip, the loudest empty promise of our age proclaims *the good life is found in your sex life*.

We unthinkingly embrace sex as our highest good because God's best gifts are what become the most alluring idols.

Instead of simply receiving good gifts from the giver of life, we look to them to *give* us life. Like the Romans rebuked by Paul, we end up worshiping and serving the created thing rather than the Creator (Rom. 1:25).

Not More *about* Sex, But More *of* Sex

We do not need to think more *about* sex; we need to think more *of* sex. We are convinced that more sex is what we need because it's such a good gift. But in so doing, we lessen its goodness and we ruin it, by asking it to deliver what only God can.

We don't value sex *enough*. In seeking the euphoria of sex outside of its rightful place, we've pursued all kinds of ruinous shortcuts such as the premature sexualization of everyone (especially little girls), sexting, pornography, hookup sex, solo sex, and I could go on. We want all the benefits of something good and hard fought without putting in the work.

But instant gratification is an imposter and a liar, especially here.

We've sold out for cheap sex, and it's left us feeling hollow. In this chapter we will confront this idol of our age, and then we'll turn to God's good design and purpose. With his help, we will lift our eyes up and off this sullied landscape and onto his truly joy-inducing blueprint, which is for our deep-down very good.

Subconscious Sexualization

Images are authoritative, as they shape our subconscious thoughts. Edward Bernays, known as the father of public relations and also the nephew of Sigmund Freud, put this reality to work in a 1920s advertising campaign for the American Tobacco Company. They wanted to increase sales to women, who were mostly secret smokers because it was stigmatized at the time. After consulting with his psychoanalyst uncle, Bernays knew he must link smoking to something bigger—to an ideal.

Bernays hired beautiful young debutantes to "smoke cigarettes while strolling in the annual Easter Sunday parade on Fifth Avenue in New York City."[1] The smoking young women were photographed by *The New York Times* and, when interviewed, said their cigarettes were, "'torches of freedom' that were 'lighting the way to the day when women would smoke on the street as casually as men.'"[2] The public internalized the clear message: smoking means youth, beauty, and equality with men. Cigarette sales soared. Sex sells.

In *American Girls: Social Media and the Secret Lives of Teenagers*, author and journalist Nancy Jo Sales says that while the majority of teen and tween girls are online for hours a day, the "online world

---

1 Robert McNamara, "Edward Bernays, Father of Public Relations and Propaganda," ThoughtCo., May 1, 2019, https://www.thoughtco.com/.
2 McNamara, "Edward Bernays."

isn't the screen of innocent fun so many parents believe it to be. It's a hypersexualized world where validation, acceptance, and worth are inexorably connected to sexual appeal and appetite."[3] One thirteen-year-old girl Sales interviewed said, "No one cares about being smart anymore. If you're beautiful, everyone will love you."[4]

This is where my momma bear hackles really start to stand up. Every woman I know can tell you something of how she was sexually conditioned, and I hate that this is my daughters' reality too. To be raised a girl in the West is to be asked when you're a seven-year-old if you have a boyfriend. It is to cruise the mall and ingest larger-than-life photos that portray nearly prepubescent girls with duck lips and desirous eyes. It is to dread reaching your twenties and having *Never Been Kissed*, as in the film starring Drew Barrymore. It is to be just twelve or thirteen and have your chest size and "doability" ranked by the boys in your school.[5] To be raised a girl in the West is to be conditioned over and over to believe that your sexuality is the most important thing about you.

Double Victimization

This cultural conditioning is the first of two victimizations that women and girls face. After the first is accomplished, the second can easily follow. Once a girl believes that her highest good is to be sexy or to have sex, she is all too willing to hand herself over to sexting, engaging with complimentary predators online, or giving into or initiating sexual acts outside of their rightful place.

3   Jaquelle Crowe Ferris, "American Girls and Their Social Media Lives," The Gospel Coalition, March 25, 2016, https://www.thegospelcoalition.org/.

4   Crowe Ferris, "American Girls."

5   Samantha Schmidt and Teddy Amenabar, "Teen Boys Rated Their Female Classmates. Readers Responded by Sharing Their Own Stories," *The Washington Post*, March 27, 2019, https://www.washingtonpost.com/.

While the first victimization happens to a girl's mind and heart, the second victimization happens to her body.

The second victimization can be unmistakable, as in the case of an assault or rape. But it is often ambiguous, as when a girl leaves an encounter wondering what just happened—she's not sure, but she knows deep down she didn't like it or want it. #MeToo reveals many women and girls are now reckoning with the oversexualization they have been subjected to for their entire lives. Sociologist and author Mary Ebberstadt says, "So socially vulnerable are these victims that they did not even know to stand up for themselves—*until an international movement gave them permission to do so.*"[6]

The first victimization has been so thorough and complete that few girls are taught they can say no to second victimization scenarios and take a different path forward. Few girls know they are worth more, worth commitment and care, and worth more than being consumed.

Hot or Not

The harmful sexualization of girls is not a distant issue happening to *those people over there*. It's everywhere, and it has repeatedly caused harm in my own community. My four daughters have gone to every kind of school imaginable both in the United States and overseas: public, private, foreign, boarding, and homeschool. In every setting (kids in Christian schools and homeschool communities are *not* immune) we've observed all kinds of unhealthy sexualization. We've seen everything from the creation of an Instagram account to rate the girls in one of our schools to boys sending nude photos of themselves and requesting nude photos of girls we personally

---

6   Mary Eberstadt, *Primal Screams: How the Sexual Revolution Created Identity Politics* (West Conshohocken, Templeton Press, 2019), 98.

know and treasure. Again, not distant kids way over there, but kids inside our own suburban Christian context.

In *American Girls*, Sales documents how girls respond to requests for nude photos. Some are flattered and think the boys really like them and so they provide them. Some are threatened with public shaming, so they provide the photos under duress. They often believe the boys when they tell them the photos will not be shared beyond their own phones. But this is almost never the case. The photos spread with the tenacity of a forest fire on parched land, significantly harming every life in their path.

A recent American Psychological Association (APA) study unsurprisingly concludes that sexualization negatively affects girls' ability to concentrate and think deeply at school, their mental health is taking a hit, they're experiencing negative physical side effects, and they're developing harmful and false ideas about their bodies, sexuality, and sex.[7]

The battle for our girls' well-being is real, as teens consume *nine hours* of entertainment media (this does not include education-related media) a day and tweens consume six.[8] The most followed women on Instagram include Ariana Grande, Kim Kardashian, Beyoncé, Jennifer Lopez, Nicki Minaj, Miley Cyrus, and Katy Perry.[9] Our girls are spending a lot of time soaking in sexualized images of women they admire and want to emulate. I'm not suggesting we allow them to follow only the Land's End Instagram account with its turtlenecks and full-coverage swimsuits, but we

7   "Report of the APA Task Force on the Sexualization of Girls," American Psychological Association, 2008, https://www.apa.org/.

8   Michael Robb, "Tweens, Teens, and Screens: What Our New Research Uncovers," *Common Sense Media*, November 2, 2015, https://www.commonsensemedia.org/.

9   Joshua Boyd, "The Top 20 Most Followed Instagram Accounts," *Brandwatch* (blog), November 11, 2020, https://www.brandwatch.com/.

have to reckon with the truth that nine hours a day of media consumption is discipling our teens (and likely you and me too).

The Porn Problem

Pornography has become a major public health concern over the last several years, and not only because of what it does to the exploited (which is obvious and well-documented) but also because of what it's doing to the consumer. The porn problem starts with the sexualization of girls (and boys too, of course, but I can cover only so much), and its foundation is the double victimization I describe above. We're grooming our girls from the youngest of ages to believe their worth is wrapped up in their sexiness.

Porn exploits both sides of the screen.

Fight the New Drug, a nonreligious, nonlegislative, nonprofit organization, says pornography harms the brain, the heart, and, really, the whole world.[10] Porn consumers suffer from higher rates of depression, anxiety, and stress, reduced cognitive functioning, less satisfaction with their sexual partners, decreased ability to perform sexually, increased negative attitudes toward women, decreased empathy for victims of sexual violence, an increase in dominating and imposing behaviors, and increased violent fantasies and actual violent behavior.[11]

A number of studies over the last few years have found that one in three women consume porn at least once a week, and about a third more consume it a couple times a month.[12] One study concludes, "Sexual arousal at the neuron level is no different between males

---

10 Home Page, Fight the New Drug (website), https://fightthenewdrug.org.

11 Overview page, Fight the New Drug (website), https://fightthenewdrug.org/overview/.

12 "Survey Finds More Than 1 in 3 Women Watch Porn at Least Once a Week," Fight the New Drug (website), February 20, 2020, https://fightthenewdrug.org/.

and females,"[13] meaning women are as at risk for becoming addicted to porn as men are, shattering generations of gender stereotypes.

Women are not only harmed by being used to make porn, but more than ever they are harmed by watching it.

Friend, if that's you, know there is help and there is hope. In my role in women's ministry, many women have come to me to confess watching porn, getting addicted to porn, or becoming addicted to solo sex. While historically it has been taboo to talk about these things, they have been historically present (with a notable increase over the last couple decades). Ellen Mary Dykas, who works with Harvest USA, a ministry focused on gospel-centered sexuality, says, "All women [experience] the impact of the fall in their sexuality. Our desires have become disordered, and our minds need transformation. Our hearts need radical reorienting toward Christ, who has called us to live fully for him and not ourselves."[14] If pornography is a stronghold for you, seek the care of a community who will express grace and truth to you, as well as provide real accountability.

And if you are a woman or girl who has been sexually assaulted, abused, or used, know that there is help and hope for you too. I have walked years with a few women who have survived such evils, and while these are often life-threatening traumas, they are not beyond repair with God's help. I see you and so does our God, who reconciles *all things* by the blood of his cross (Col. 1:20). Please seek the help of a trusted Christian counselor, support group, and life-giving friends right away. You are not meant to pursue healing alone, and there are trained women who stand ready to help.

13 "Survey Finds," https://fightthenewdrug.org/.
14 Gloria Furman and Kathleen Nielson, ed., *Word-Filled Women's Ministry: Loving and Serving the Church* (Wheaton, IL: Crossway, 2015), 182–83.

Hooking Up, More or Less

It used to be that if you wanted to have a sexual encounter—
to hook up—you had to go out and meet someone at a frat party, or
cocktail party, or wherever. But that's no longer the case. Hooking
up has never been as efficient and as easy as it is today. Teens, young
adults, and even the middle-aged and retirees (it's true, there are
several apps just for people over sixty-five), increasingly find one
another online, swipe right, and exchange enough information to
find a time and a place to have a sexual encounter.

With more than 50 million active Tinder profiles, 30 billion
matches have been made on that app alone. And there are over
1,500 other dating apps available for download.[15] Of course, not
all of them are intended to lead solely to a sexual encounter alone,
but some of the most popular ones are. Most millennials, and for
sure those who make up GenZ or iGen (people born from the
mid-1990s through the mid-2010s), would much rather communicate with a screen than with an actual human. "We hook up
because we have no social skills. We have no social skills because we
hook up," is how one college student put it.[16] Negotiating sex via
an app takes less time, less social finesse, less mystery, less money,
less emotional investment, less of everything, really, if a physical
encounter is all you're after.

The downsides are predictable: many women report enduring
painful, even violent, and confusingly nonconsensual sex as a result
of these encounters.[17] Others report needing to get really drunk to

15 Terry Stancheva, "How Many People Are on Tinder in 2020?," *TechJury* (blog), July 28,
    2020, https://techjury.net/blog/.
16 Kate Julian, "Why Are Young People Having So Little Sex?," *The Atlantic*, December 2018,
    https://www.theatlantic.com/magazine/.
17 Julian, "Why Are Young People Having So Little Sex?"

endure the awkwardness of it all, and there's a general consensus amongst young people that no relationship or even conversation should be expected alongside or as a result of the hookup.[18]

The very latest research, though, is likely something you didn't see coming. Teens and young adults are now having *less* sex, not *more*, than previous generations. Referred to as the Sex Recession, the percentage of high school students who have had sex dropped from 54 percent to 40 percent from 1991 to 2017.[19] GenZ is on track to have fewer sexual partners than both GenX and the Baby Boomers.[20]

Everyone's immediate response to the Sex Recession is: *Good! Isn't that what we want?* And to be sure, less illicit sex is a good thing. But the reality behind less hooking up is not more wholesome and healthy attitudes about sex. Rather, it's a new iteration in the pursuit of satisfying selfish lust.[21] We are becoming so driven by selfish desires and self-satisfaction, so consumed with individual autonomy over communal good, that the real act of sex may soon be antiquated. As I said, our culture does not need to think more *about* sex, we need to think more *of* sex.

Most of us have never learned the glory, wonder, and joy of God's design for our sexuality. We suspect his design is old-fashioned and oppressive. We think he's holding out on us, a cosmic killjoy. We assume the world knows better.

---

18 Nancy Pearcey, *Love Thy Body* (Grand Rapids, MI: Baker, 2018), 119–20.

19 "Trends in the Prevalence of Sexual Behaviors and HIV Testing National YRBS: 1991—2015," Center for Disease Control, Division of Adolescent and School Health, https://www.cdc.gov/.

20 Jean M. Twenge, "Have Smartphones Destroyed a Generation?," *The Atlantic*, September 2017, https://www.theatlantic.com/.

21 Carl Trueman, *The Rise and Triumph of the Modern Self: Cultural Amnesia, Expressive Individualism, and the Road to the Sexual Revolution* (Wheaton, IL: Crossway, 2020), 291.

We are embodied souls and, therefore, our sex lives are our spiritual lives. By settling for the world's view of sex, we have harmed ourselves and each other. Are we willing to trust the Lord with his design?

First, a Caution about Abuse

Before we dive into God's design for sex and marriage, I want to acknowledge with compassion and clarity that "on average, more than one in three women in the US will experience rape, physical violence, and/or stalking by an intimate partner."[22] Abuse in marriage and intimate relationships is a heartbreaking and horrific reality. Please know that the following paragraphs about God's intention for marriages to be unbroken and self-sacrificial are written with nonabusive relationships in mind. Physical, sexual, and emotional abuse in marriage is wrong and an abhorrent deviation from God's good design. If you are a woman who has or is experiencing abuse, please seek the care of a trained and compassionate counselor who can help you navigate the intricacies of your situation. I pray that you are part of a church family who sees you and serves you. My heart goes out to you, and I want you to hear that God's design is in no way for you to remain in the hands of your abuser. Reader, as we progress, know this discussion assumes a nonabsuive situation.

Marriage Is God's Idea, Not Ours

In the twenty-first century we see marriage (and sex and sexuality) as an individual expression—our idea, ours to manipulate and change and legalize in whatever ways we see fit. But the origin and purpose

22 "Domestic Violence Statistics," National Domestic Violence Hotline, 2021, https://www.thehotline.org/stakeholders/domestic-violence-statistics/.

of marriage is found in creation itself, put there by our Creator. The Bible begins and ends with two weddings, and we who follow Christ are referred to as his bride throughout.

The first mention of sex and marriage in the Bible is in Genesis 2, when God said, "Therefore a man shall leave his father and his mother and hold fast to his wife, and they shall become one flesh" (Gen. 2:24). In their book *The Meaning of Marriage*, pastor Tim Keller and his wife Kathy say that "one-flesh" phrase points to more than a physical union. It "is a union between two people so profound that they virtually become a new, single person. The word 'united' . . . means 'to make a binding covenant or contract.'"[23] Sex is the physical sign and means of creating a union that goes way beyond physicality and is not meant to be broken apart.

The last place we see marriage in the Bible is at the very other end, in the book of Revelation, where it says we who are followers of Jesus Christ will be his bride and he will be our bridegroom. One day you and I who trust Jesus as our Savior will be eternally unified with him in heaven. At what the Bible calls the marriage supper of the Lamb, there will be a multitude rejoicing: "Hallelujah! . . . for the marriage of the Lamb has come, and his Bride has made herself ready; it was granted her to clothe herself with fine linen, bright and pure" (Rev. 19:6–8). You and I will be the bride clothed in white—pure, because Jesus has paid for our sins and clothes us in his righteousness instead.

If you've heard that Jesus says we will not be married in heaven (Matt. 22:30) and you've wondered why, here's your answer. We'll no longer be married to our human spouses because we will be married to Jesus.

---

23 Timothy Keller with Kathy Keller, *The Meaning of Marriage: Facing the Complexities of Commitment with the Wisdom of God* (New York: Dutton, 2011), 222–23.

I realize how very strange that sounds. Trying to wrap our finite human minds around this otherworldly reality is probably futile. C. S. Lewis's oft-quoted illustration is helpful here. We are "like an ignorant child who wants to go on making mud pies in a slum because he cannot imagine what is meant by the offer of a holiday at the sea."[24] We just don't yet have eyes or understanding for the sea, when we are here, surrounded by the slums.

Sex and Marriage Preach the Gospel

Thankfully, the apostle Paul offers us some insight. He calls this theological reality a *mega-mysterion*, a mystery or sort of wonderful secret through which God reveals himself and his purposes.[25] Quoting Genesis 2 Paul says, "'Therefore a man shall leave his father and mother and hold fast to his wife, and the two shall become one flesh.' This mystery is profound, and I am saying that it refers to Christ and the church" (Eph. 5:31–32).

The gospel and marriage illuminate one another.

Marriage was made to represent the love, commitment, and sacrifice of God toward his people. If you are married, your marriage is a physical display to the world that Jesus is forever, unbreakably committed to his people.

This is a big deal. This is why it matters who and what we believe about sex. The gravest consequence of our flippancy about sex is that it mars the symbol God created to communicate how he will never leave us and never forsake us (Deut. 31:6; Heb. 13:5). God's boundaries for sex are not old-fashioned or oppressive. He is not a killjoy, and he is not after our moralism or performative good behavior. He's after his own glory, and he's after what's best for you and me.

24 C. S. Lewis, *The Weight of Glory and Other Addresses* (New York: Macmillan, 1949), 2.
25 Keller and Keller, *The Meaning of Marriage*, 45.

We commit violence against our God and his people when we think too little of sex. This is not about fretting about purity or chastity or following a list of rules. This is about living according to reality because that's what is best for all of us. God, our Maker, can be trusted. As your Creator and mine, he really does know and want our very best.

To Covenant and Not Consume

Understanding that our marriages—which really means our engagement in sex, too, because this is what is meant by *one flesh*—are meant to display God's love to the world changes everything. The gospel does that. Following Jesus radically reorders everything about us.

Christ calls us to be *covenant makers* rather than *consuming takers*.

Sex is not wrong or taboo in God's eyes—it's a gift, designed by him, for his glory and our good. And within marriage, he commands it. Sex is designed to be a vulnerable act of handing oneself over to another. It is to say, without shame, *I am yours and you are mine*. All of me for all of you. God knows we are continuously tempted to be selfish, in sex and otherwise, and so he commands, "The husband should give to his wife her conjugal rights, and likewise the wife to her husband. For the wife does not have authority over her own body, but the husband does. Likewise the husband does not have authority over his own body, but the wife does. Do not deprive one another, except perhaps by agreement for a limited time, that you may devote yourselves to prayer" (1 Cor. 7:3–5).

Tim and Kathy Keller say, "Sex is for whole-life self-giving. However, the sinful heart wants to use sex for selfish reasons, not self-giving, and therefore the Bible puts many rules around it to direct us to use it the right way."[26] This is why sex is reserved for marriage. We are

---

26 Keller and Keller, *The Meaning of Marriage*, 220–21.

not meant to enter into a one-flesh union with anyone with whom we have not already fully committed ourselves in every other way.

When my husband and I provide premarital counseling, we always tell couples that marriage is not a fifty-fifty endeavor. The world says, *I'll do half and you do half, and we'll be happy.* But it never works out like that, because your 50 percent will always look bigger and better than your spouse's. Anytime we keep score, we are the winner. Instead, marriage must be a one hundred-one hundred kind of commitment. Both spouses, with God's help, must strive to give each other 100 percent of themselves. Covenanting over consuming is no easy thing.

Jesus poured himself out for you and me, and he asks husbands and wives to do the same for one another. It's a sacrificial commitment, not a feeling, not a sentimentality, not a passion. It's a choice, a walk of obedience, a begging of God's help to obey him and love one another above ourselves.

This kind of commitment is ultimately freeing, as each spouse knows he or she can depend on the other. This kind of commitment makes marriages stronger in the face of temptations. When we have a robust reason—namely, that Jesus laid down his life for me while I was still a sinner (Rom. 5:8), therefore I can lay down my life for my spouse while he or she is still a sinner—we are more likely to persevere. "We love because he first loved us" (1 John 4:19). Remembering the cross, Jesus's death on our behalf, and his miraculous resurrection frees us from selfishness and propels us to be more like our Savior.

The Bible tells us "God is love" (1 John 4:8). We would do well then to recognize that "God knows far more about love than we do."[27] His design for sex is for our good, for our thriving.

---

27 Sam Allberry, "Where to Find Hope and Help amid the Sexual Revolution," The Gospel Coalition, November 5, 2018, https://www.thegospelcoalition.org/.

Let's Seek What Satisfies

In the story of the prodigal son the older brother specifies what his younger brother's reckless living is. He says the younger brother spent all their father's money on prostitutes (Luke 15:30). He may or may not have been exaggerating, but it's not hard to imagine that reckless living in the first century or the twenty-first century is a sort of euphemism for seeking to satiate oneself with a lot of sex and sexual partners.

As you know, the Prodigal Son came to himself and realized he was perishing. Can you see us in this story too? In this chapter we've only taken a glimpse of the perishing caused by our reckless living: the declining mental health of girls, the despair and addiction caused by pornography, the drunkenness needed to hook up, the real and heavy loneliness that comes from sexual sin. But just as the Prodigal came to himself and went home, so can we.

No matter how we have sold ourselves out for cheap sex—and we *all* have in one way or another (Matt. 5:28; 1 John 1:10)—the Father waits, even now, with his robes hiked up, ready to run and embrace you and me.

Can you just imagine how different *The Bachelor* and *The Bachelorette* would be if all of the participants knew their worth and value as humans made in God's image? What if they knew God would never leave them or forsake them? What if they didn't clamor for approval and acceptance through romance and sex on public display? What if they all rejected one another's empty promises and instead embraced the goodness of our God?

Friends, *we have a Father.* We are sons and daughters and heirs through God (Gal. 4:7). Why do we insist on perishing out here, while he awaits at home with a feast? Our good God "satisfies the longing soul, / and the hungry soul he fills with good things" (Ps.

107:9). Jesus is the bread of life—if we come to him, we will never hunger and never thirst (John 6:35). It's never too late, and you're never too far, to return home.

God's desire is for your good. His will is that you would thrive. He died for you and me! He's not grumpy or selfish or holding out on us. Rather, he's holding out abundant life for those who believe. We have a choice: Will we follow the world and keep giving into the cultural counterfeit or will we surrender to the real deal?

Isaiah puts the question to us like this:

Why do you spend your money for that which is not bread,
    and your labor for that which does not satisfy?
Listen diligently to me, and eat what is good,
    and delight yourselves in rich food.
Incline your ear, and come to me;
    hear, that your soul may live." (Isa. 55:2–3)

Home is where the feast is. Home is where you and I will find soul-deep satisfaction. Home is where we are safe, adored, protected, cherished. When we sell out for cheap sex, we harm ourselves and one another. But we were made for so much more.

Discussion Questions

1. Just to break the ice and share a laugh before we dive into the heavy truths in this chapter, tell your group an awkward or hilarious dating story about you or someone you know.

2. Have you observed or personally experienced the sexual conditioning of girls? Can anything be done to combat that subconscious conditioning in ourselves and other girls?

3. Talk about how pornography exploits both sides of the screen. What are the dangers of consuming porn? Is your women's ministry or community a safe place to confess sexting, porn consumption, solo sex, and other taboo sins? What about a safe place to come forward as a sexual abuse survivor? What can you personally do to make your community more transparent? Take a minute to share resources with each other, so that women who might need help now or in the future might know where to go.

4. Are you surprised that many Christians believe and follow the world rather than God when it comes to sex? Do you think you have done that too? Are you willing to trust the Lord with his design? Reflect on the *mega-mysterion* in Ephesians 5:31–32.

5. What is the difference in marriage (or any sexual relationship) when you choose to covenant rather than consume?

6. Read Romans 5:8 and 1 John 4:19 and share how remembering the cross, Jesus's death on our behalf, and his miraculous resurrection, frees us from selfishness and propels us to be more like our Savior. Close by praying and asking the Lord to help you love others because he first loved you.

6

Abortion Has Not Delivered

"AS LONG AS THE GOVERNMENT doesn't tell me what to do with my body," my friend brooded. I remember the moment clearly. A group of my college girlfriends and I were gathered after lunch, shooting the breeze until our afternoon classes.

Yeah, I thought, *that's really true. I don't want the government controlling my body either. How scary would that be?* When the government exerts control over people's bodies, bad things happen. *She's right*, was the extent of my inward wrestling. To be sure, I didn't like the idea of ending a baby's life, but the thought of our government having tyranny over my body and my friends' bodies seemed worse. Sometimes that hard choice would have to be made, I reasoned, in order to protect our greater freedom.

I was won over in a flash by a pithy saying. There was no competing voice in my head, no alternate sound bite for me to measure against this one. *My body, my choice* was ubiquitous in my spheres, and it took root with ease. And yes, I was a Christian at the time.

While that moment was solidifying, it was preceded by a lifetime that prepared me to embrace it. My girlfriends and I were raised to believe that we alone would command our destinies. If we dreamed it, we would achieve it. And we would not tolerate a boyfriend or government or baby who might derail us.

A Necessary Choice

I had seen abortion up close in high school. One lunch hour we were gathered in the school parking lot, paper Burger King sacks in hand. A carful of friends pulled up to say they wouldn't be back. They had to, you know, *take care of things*. We nodded knowingly. One passenger was pregnant and didn't want to be. The other girls were going along for moral support. Her mom knew. It was for the best, everyone agreed.

That sad, but *so normal*, scenario played out more than once amongst my peers and friends back then. We didn't question the morality of it. We didn't wonder if it was really best. We believed it was required. Motherhood at that moment was so far out, no one ever considered it a possibility.

Abortion was assumed. Sure, it was unfortunate, but that was mostly because we heard it was painful and would require a few days at home to recover. We knew our friends would be a little sad afterward. But we were sure it was necessary. And so did the 1,221,585 women and girls who received a legal abortion in 1996, the year I graduated from high school.[1]

Exploitation, Not Liberation

Twenty-five years later, in May 2021, Dallas high school valedictorian Paxton Smith took the stage to address her graduating class

---

1 Lisa M. Koonin, M.N., M.P.H. ed., "Abortion Surveillance—United States, 1996, Morbidity and Mortality Weekly Report," Centers for Disease Control and Prevention, July 30, 1999, https://www.cdc.gov/.

and all of their loved ones who had gathered for the celebration. She pulled a speech from inside her gown and used her moment on stage to protest a newly passed law in Texas, which outlawed abortion after the detection of a fetal heartbeat.

Smith said, "I have dreams and hopes and ambitions. Every girl graduating today does. And we have spent our entire lives working towards our future. . . . I am terrified that if my contraceptives fail, I am terrified that if I am raped, then my hopes and aspirations and dreams and efforts for my future will no longer matter . . . there is a war on my body and a war on my rights. A war on the rights of your mothers, a war on the rights of your sisters, a war on the rights of your daughters."[2]

Met with cheers, Smith's message was clear: without the right to an abortion, girls' futures are hopeless. If they cannot end unwanted pregnancies, women cannot reach their potential. Without choice, dreams and goals will go unrealized.

Her brief speech was a resounding echo of popular thinking: abortion is liberation.

But popular thinking is not necessarily right thinking. Human well-being requires harmony with reality. And what's true is that abortion demeans, uses, and ultimately harms women. We were raised to believe it was for our good, that it would deliver us the autonomy and success we deserve, that it would truly set us free. In truth, however, abortion has done the very opposite.

Under the guise of empowerment, women have instead been made vulnerable. My college days' conclusion was naive. I now want so much more for women. Abortion sells us way short; we will see that in the history and sociological data that follow.

---

2 Bill Chappell, "High School Valedictorian Swaps Speech to Speak Out against Texas' New Abortion Law," *National Public Radio*, June 3, 2021, https://www.npr.org/.

I promise, there is real hope in the final pages of this chapter. If you are a woman who has chosen abortion, please keep reading. I know many of you deeply and personally, and I've had your stories on my heart and your faces on my mind as I've written these words. Read the truth about our fallen world, the lies you and I believed, and the hope we mistakenly put in ourselves. Read the truth about the harm "choice" has inflicted on us, our children, and society as a whole. And then read with deep relief and great joy that that's not the end of your story or anyone's story. Read about our God who forgives and makes all things new. His design for us is glorious and good, so far beyond the fraud of abortion.

Femaleness Deemed a Liability

The legalization of abortion is just one part of a broader cultural picture. The Sexual Revolution—while a massive and abrupt so-cietal shift itself—was born out of a long sequence of changes that prioritized the autonomous self above communal good, as we saw in chapter 2. The advent of the birth control pill and no-fault divorce worked together to unhinge sex from the consequence of pregnancy and the context of marriage.

But here's what we take for granted today when we talk about contraception: the pill was made for women. Since its advent, contraception has been the burden of females, not males. Women ingest it; women are affected by it. It's the female body that is deemed broken, out of alignment, in need of fixing.

Whether it was for expediency or by design or subconsciously, we collectively labeled the male body normal, preferred, just fine the way it is. It was the woman's body that needed to be changed, her biology altered, not his. The cry for equality in second-wave feminism was a declaration that female physiology is a problem and the solution is found in having a body that can function more like a man's.

How might history be different if instead in that moment we stood with our Maker and proclaimed the female body to be very good? What if, instead of suppressing what women can do, we celebrated it? What if, instead of preventing pregnancy, we protected it? What if we swapped out inconvenience for awe?

We know what actually happened, though. In the quest for unfettered sex, we began sacrificing both women and children. Rather than adjusting the male body, or better yet, our society—our values, our appetites, our threshold for legalized violence—we legalized abortion.

Enshrined in Law

At the age of twenty-one, Norma McCorvey was pregnant with her third child. She wanted an abortion, but it was not legal in Texas in 1969 unless it was to save the life of the mother. After seeking an illegal abortion at an unlawful clinic and finding that it had recently shut down, she began working with an adoption attorney to prepare for the birth of her child. Incidentally, her attorney connected her to a lawyer who was preparing to challenge Texas abortion law.

McCorvey was given the alias of Jane Roe (the Roe in *Roe v. Wade*), and a suit was filed in her name against Dallas County District Attorney Henry Wade (the Wade in *Roe v. Wade*). McCorvey never appeared in court, never testified, and didn't necessarily want abortion to be widely legalized—she just wanted one herself.

Ultimately, on January 23, 1973, the Supreme Court issued a 7–2 decision in favor of Jane Roe, legalizing abortion across the nation. The justices determined that women have a fundamental right to choose to end their own pregnancies, without excessive government restriction. They reasoned that outlawing abortion infringed upon a pregnant woman's right to privacy, because of the distress and difficulties associated with an unwanted or unplanned child.

In the duration of the case, McCorvey delivered her baby and placed him or her for adoption. She never did have an abortion.

In a surprising and widely unknown turn of events, after working in an abortion clinic and witnessing firsthand for the first time its impact on women, McCorvey rejected the abortion rights movement and went to work in a pro-life pregnancy resource center instead. In 2005, before the Senate Judiciary Committee she provided this testimony:

> I believe that I was used and abused by the court system in America. Instead of helping women in Roe v. Wade, I brought destruction to me and millions of women throughout the nation. . . . Instead of getting me financial or vocational help, instead of helping me to get off of drugs and alcohol, instead of working for open adoption or giving me other help, my lawyers . . . were looking for a young, white woman to be a guinea pig for a great new social experiment. . . . Do you have any idea how much emotional grief I have experienced? It is like a living hell knowing that you have had a part to play, though in some sense I was just a pawn of the legal system.[3]

Are Unborn Babies Persons?

At the heart of the *Roe v. Wade* decision was a prevailing, albeit likely subconscious, society-wide assumption that we define ourselves. We have increasingly believed over the last century that our identity, our reality, who we really are, is self-invented and self-realized. In

3   Norma McCorvey, "Testimony of Norma McCorvey," June 23, 2005, https://www.judiciary .senate.gov/imo/media/doc/McCorvey%20Testimony%20062305.pdf.

1973 women gained the right to abort because they did not define themselves as mothers.

Never mind that the babies existed. Never mind that the women were actually pregnant. Feelings, not facts, would shape reality.

The majority opinion, written by Justice Harry Blackmun, says "The word 'person,' as used in the Fourteenth Amendment, does not include the unborn. . . . If the suggestion of personhood is established . . . the fetus' right to life would then be guaranteed."[4] Unborn babies, he reasoned, might be humans, but they are not persons because they have no ability to self-define. Breathing in and breathing out the cultural air of the day, the Supreme Court ruled that a person is someone who defines his or her own existence. To be a person, one must be able to *think* not just to *be*.[5]

Dualism: Body and Mind

It follows from this worldview, then, that an abortion is an act of the body and bears no consequence on the mind. We think there should be no mental or emotional fallout from an abortion because we are not our bodies. And further, we can end an unborn life without any ill effects, because it's just a human, not a person. It isn't harmful because aborted fetuses are just bodies.

This philosophy of personhood has real consequences. To date, over 60 million women in America have made a choice about who they want to be and inflicted that choice on their own bodies and their babies' bodies.[6] Abortion clinic counselors tell women every day that abortion is a good option. They say it's safe, it's not too

4   Roe v. Wade, 410 U.S. 113 (1973).
5   I am indebted to author and philosopher Nancy Pearcey who gives this dualism thorough treatment in her book *Love Thy Body* (Grand Rapids, MI: Baker, 2018).
6   "Reported Annual Abortions 1973–2017," National Right to Life Educational Foundation, 2018, https://nrlc.org/uploads/factsheets/FS01AbortionintheUS.pdf.

painful, it's emotionally less damaging than birthing the baby. Women with unplanned pregnancies are convinced the physical act will not hurt their immaterial hearts and souls.

But what has been lauded as an empowering choice since 1973 has proven to be a devastating regret. The victims of abortion are not just the children. They are also the mothers who believe the abortion counselors, their partners and friends and family, and a culture that says, *You have to do this. It's for the best. It's not a person anyway. You can eliminate this mistake and move on with your life like it never happened. You can employ and celebrate choice to determine your destiny.*

Abortion: The Data

A half century after its legalization, we must finally and fully admit that abortion is a cultural counterfeit, an empty promise. What follows is not an exhaustive account of all the ill effects of abortion, but hopefully it's an enlightening one. I'll warn you now that it's likely to be a disheartening read. As a people we are not generally open and honest about the dismal realities of abortion. This is heavy stuff.

So here's what we must remember: "The light shines in the darkness, and the darkness has not overcome it" (John 1:5). We have to be honest and real about what's dark, so that light might shine. Jesus is the light of the world. He is victorious and alive. He is the giver of life. Even the darkness of abortion cannot overcome him.

My desire is that women would know more than pithy sound bites and stand ready with the truth so that we might offer real hope to ourselves, our sisters, our girlfriends, our daughters, and any stranger on the street who doesn't know what to do with the unplanned child in her womb.

Abortion debases genuine feminism. Nobody inside the movement says that abortion destroys "just a clump of cells" anymore.

Bioethicists, doctors, counselors, and activists all know that an embryo is an actual baby. One Feminist for Life said that to link feminism with abortion is to create "terrorist feminism" because it forces the feminist to be "willing to kill for the cause you believe in."[7] Whereas the original feminists protected women and children, were antislavery activists, social reformers, and suffragists, second-wave feminism cannot be separated from killing.

Most women feel pressured into abortion, unprepared for it, and guilty about it. One study reveals the following about post-abortive women in America:[8]

- More than 90 percent said they weren't given enough information to make an informed choice.
- More than 80 percent said they probably would not have aborted if they hadn't been so heavily encouraged to do so.
- Eighty-three percent said they would have carried to term if they had had more support in their lives.

Abortion greatly increases women's mental health risks. A *British Journal of Psychiatry* study found that abortion causes:[9]

- 81 percent increase in risk of mental health conditions;
- 34 percent increase in risk of anxiety;

7   Randy Alcorn, "It Is Possible to Be a Feminist and Be Prolife," *Eternal Perspective Ministries* (blog), June 11, 2018, https://www.epm.org/blog/.

8   "Key Facts about Abortion," Elliot Institute, n.d., www.afterabortion.org, as quoted in Randy Alcorn, *Why Pro-Life?: Caring for the Unborn and Their Mothers* (Peabody, MA: Hendrickson, 2012), 77.

9   Priscilla K. Coleman, "Abortion and Mental Health: Quantitative Synthesis and Analysis of Research Published 1995–2009," Cambridge University Press, January 2, 2018, https://www.cambridge.org/core/.

- 37 percent increase in risk of depression;
- 110 percent increase in risk of alcohol use;
- 155 percent increase in risk of suicide.

Women seek abortions for reasons that might be alleviated with other social services and supports. According to Care Net, an umbrella organization for thousands of pregnancy resource centers, women are abortion-minded for the following reasons:[10]

- financial (40 percent)
- timing (36 percent)
- partner-related reasons (31 percent)
- the need to focus on other children (29 percent)
- multiple reasons (64 percent)
- a recent traumatic event such as unemployment, a breakup, or falling behind on rent or mortgage (57 percent)
- a physical problem with their health (12 percent)
- rape (1 percent)
- incest (<0.5 percent)

Abortion has a racist past and a racist present. Margaret Sanger founded Planned Parenthood and championed birth control in the early 1900s. Sanger's motives were racist and rooted in the eugenics movement, whose motto was, "More from the fit, less from the unfit." While I am confident that the majority of Planned Parenthood employees are not now intentionally racist, current abortion numbers as related to race should cause a public outcry.

10 Care Net, "Facts on Abortion," 2019, https://cdn2.hubspot.net/hubfs/367552/Downloads/Top_40_Abortion_Statistics.pdf.

Abortion is responsible for 61 percent of black American deaths, and 64 percent of Hispanic/Latino deaths.[11] While black Americans make up only 13 percent of the US population, black women account for 36 percent of all abortions.[12] These gross imbalances should give every American pause. Why do we allow abortion providers to prey on women of color?

Let me be very clear: these statistics are not because black or Hispanic/Latino women are more selfish or more violent. It's because they, like all of us, have been shaped by a culture and a context that says abortion is better for you than a baby. For women with fewer resources, as minority women in the United States often are, abortion often feels like the only way forward.

We *all* need to be asking ourselves what we're doing to equip women in need. How can we join women on the margins of society so that abortion does not feel like their best option?

At-Home Abortions

The overall number of abortions in the United States is in decline, which is likely due to an increase in contraception use, the Sex Recession discussed in chapter 5, and the underreporting of at-home abortions (discussed below). The most recent year for which United States abortion statistics are available (2017) reveals that the lives of 862,000 babies were ended in that year alone.[13] This "reduced" number is still tragic and does not include a comprehensive count

11 Danny David, "Study: Abortion Is the Leading Cause of Death in America," *Live Action News*, August 11, 2016, https://www.liveaction.org/news/unc-study-demonstrates-effect-of-abortion-on-minorities-and-public-health/.

12 Centers for Disease Control and Prevention, "Abortion Surveillance — United States, 2014," November 24, 2017, https://www.cdc.gov/mmwr/volumes/66/ss/ss6624a1.htm.

13 "Induced Abortion in the United States, Fact Sheet," Guttmacher Institute, September 2019, https://www.guttmacher.org/fact-sheet/induced-abortion-united-states.

of medication-induced abortions, which are increasingly routine but hard to track.

The increasing availability of abortions at home makes confronting the counterfeit of abortion feel more urgent than ever. Abortion by medication is currently available to women through abortion clinics, their doctors, and the mail via telemedicine or an internet order. In 2023, by law, public university campus clinics in California will begin offering medication-induced abortions to their students (the morning-after pill, which is different than a medication abortion, is already available in vending machines on campuses across the country).

A woman who ends her pregnancy by medication first ingests a pill containing mifepristone to deplete her body of progesterone, which is needed to support a pregnancy. The following day the woman takes a pill containing misoprostol, which induces miscarriage. The seeming ease and anonymity have made the process attractive, but it remains very dangerous. Women experience cramping (oftentimes extreme and debilitating), hemorrhaging, and the delivery of a dead baby. Although Planned Parenthood pressures women to ingest the first pill before they leave their offices, all of this can happen in the privacy of their own home (or maybe the not-so-private dormitory bathroom), which means women and girls are further isolated and at risk both physically and emotionally with these so-called self-managed abortions. Allowing a woman to endure such risk and trauma alone should be unthinkable. In what other sphere of medicine is this even imaginable?

Women and their babies deserve so much more.

Created to Be Subcreators

Abortion, we're told, is a choice. Who doesn't love choice? But this choice is different. Choosing to snuff out a life in the womb puts us in the seat of the Sovereign, a position we cannot handle. Our hearts are not meant to bear the weight of deciding who gets to live and who has to die. It breaks us when we do.

It is plain to see that the female body is meant to bring forth and nurture life, not end it. We have a womb. We have mammary glands. We are born carrying eggs. Our bodies proclaim that we are to reproduce, to nurture and nourish children. It's not the sum total of the female purpose, but it's undeniable that we are life-givers by design.

Bringing new life into the world is a shockingly marvelous gift. It's awe-inspiring. Women have a huge privilege in being subcreators with God.[14] Our bodies are not liabilities. The female body is glorious and good and worth protecting and cherishing.

Abortion, therefore, inflicts a primal wound. While proponents laud the procedure as a quick fix and simple solution, the reality is that it impacts not only our bodies but our hearts and souls as well. To kill the child inside us does violence to our composition as women. It contradicts reality; it goes against our very nature.

Abortion *demands* life, but we are meant to *give* life. We will never be okay aborting a baby, because we were made in the image of a God who gave his own life for our sake. When we image him, we sacrifice ourselves for others, and we thrive.

We All Bear the Blame

Abortion is a heartbreaking reality that never had to be. I'm moved to tears as I think of many dear friends and the numerous women I've counseled who chose abortion because they thought they had to.

14 Timothy Keller, *On Birth* (New York City: Penguin, 2020), 7.

We must acknowledge that we as a people have made murder appear more appealing than motherhood. *The blame for abortion lies with all of us.*

Abortion has served as a quick fix for a society that pursues sex without consequence and prioritizes the male body and function above the female. Rather than conforming societal values and expectations to the good and awe-inspiring design of women and what we contribute to society through fertility and reproduction, we have instead been asked and convinced to sacrifice ourselves and our babies.

We've settled, advocated even, for this messed-up way of life. And there have been way too many victims. So how do we move forward? How does a post-abortive woman move past her regret and trauma? How do we all forge a new normal for women and girls?

Abortion Is Not Unforgivable

The wounds endured by a post-abortive woman are unlike any other. As described in the statistics above, they are soul-deep and cause seemingly insurmountable shame and regret. The father of lies (John 8:44), Satan, whispers to women that abortion in unforgivable, but that's not true.

Our God stands ready and eager to forgive and to free.

A post-abortive woman must first acknowledge the choice she made. While it's true that many others are culpable, a post-abortive woman cannot move forward unless she is honest with herself and her God. The apostle Paul says, "Godly grief produces a repentance that leads to salvation without regret, whereas worldly grief produces death" (2 Cor. 7:10). Worldly grief keeps a woman in bondage; it produces death because it is not honest, contrite, or broken before God. But godly grief owns sin, acknowledges wrongdoing, and lays it all before the Lord for his forgiveness and healing.

The sin of abortion was paid for, once and for all, on the cross. Do not believe the lie that Jesus's death was not payment enough.

The truth is, "If we confess our sins, he is faithful and just to forgive us our sins and to cleanse us from all unrighteousness" (1 John 1:9). If you confess your role in abortion, Jesus will not only forgive you, but *cleanse* you.

The Bible says, "As high as the heavens are above the earth, / so great is [God's] steadfast love toward those who fear him; / as far as the east is from the west, / so far does he remove our transgressions from us" (Ps. 103:11–12). As you and I fear the Lord—as we revere him, acknowledge his holiness and our sin—*all* of our transgressions will be removed from us forever.

Experiencing the peace that comes from God's complete forgiveness is rarely a one-and-done event. Christ-centered counseling and post-abortion support groups are invaluable. Many women find it healing to share their stories and to provide care to pregnant women in crisis at pregnancy resource centers.

The very good and final news for post-abortive women is this: "If the Son sets you free, you will be free indeed" (John 8:36). No matter the sin, no one can take away the forgiveness bought for us at the cross of Christ. Further, no one can take the freedom wrought in his resurrection. Because Jesus lives, we will too (John 14:19).

Do You Really Want to be Inclusive?

Author and philosopher Nancy Pearcey says, "The pro-choice position is exclusive. It says that some people don't measure up. They don't make the cut. They don't qualify for the rights of personhood.

[But] the pro-life position is inclusive. If you are a member of the human race, you're 'in.'"[15]

You're in. I'm in. Every man, woman, and child is in. Every life is a treasure to protect.

While it's true that over 60 million babies have been aborted in the United States since 1973, with a move of God's Spirit amongst his people, this can become a reflection of history rather than a forecast of the future. There are currently over 2,700 pregnancy resource centers in the United States,[16] while there are only around eight hundred abortion clinics.[17]

I have served in a few pregnancy resource centers and have sat across from women as they've weighed their options. They each have a unique story, but so many are vulnerable because they lack an education, a job, a supportive partner, a healthy homelife. Many women face real danger, abuse, and shame at home. Providing resources and care can make all the difference. Walking them through steps such as finding a Medicaid-approved doctor, getting help with groceries, getting matched with a mentoring mom, and more can make the difference between life and death.

What if, with God's help, we took him seriously? What if, with the empowerment of the Holy Spirit, we the church laid ourselves down for others? What if we took the tangible goodness of our God to women in need? What if we pursued life and the well-being of others with such tenacity that abortion became unnecessary, unthinkable even?

The pro-life community must come to realize that this is not an "us versus them" situation. *They* are *us*. As humans we are in this

---

15 Nancy Pearcey, *Love Thy Body* (Grand Rapids, MI: Baker, 2018), 64.

16 Nicole Stacy, "Pro-life Pregnancy Centers Served 2 Million People, Saved Communities $161M in 2017," Charlotte Lozier Institute, September 5, 2018, https://lozierinstitute.org/.

17 "Data Center," Guttmacher Institute, accessed April 20, 2020, https://data.guttmacher.org /states/table?state=US&topics=57&dataset=data.

together. How can we all choose life together, so that our children may live (Deut. 30:19)?

This is the biblical worldview, which is truly inclusive, in action.

Going Home

In 2020 FX debuted a documentary on the life of Norma Mc-Corvey, called *AKA Jane Roe*. Filmmaker Nicholas Sweeney says McCorvey reached out to him to make a deathbed confession. She wanted the world to know before she died that her pro-life work was a fraud. In the film she says, "I think it was a mutual thing. You know, I took their money, and they put me out in front of the cameras and told me what to say."[18]

Critics of the film say Sweeney didn't press McCorvey enough to uncover what's true. Many conclude that the real Norma McCorvey was never revealed, that her own words were unconvincing. Perhaps she herself never felt at peace in the pro-choice movement *or* the pro-life movement and was always treated as a pawn. She always wanted to be an actress, she told Sweeney.

It's devastating to realize that Jane Roe was most likely played first by abortion activists and then perhaps by pro-life activists too. Maybe she liked the spotlight or maybe she just didn't know better how to navigate her own life. Either way, she's now an emblem of the greater exploitation of women and girls during her lifetime. Either way, her tragic legacy confirms for us that without a firm foundation and a supportive community, vulnerable women and girls are likely to be used by the world around them.

---

18 Alisa Chang, "New FX Documentary Explores Life of the Woman Behind Roe v. Wade Decision," "All Things Considered," National Public Radio, May 22, 2020, https://www .npr.org/.

This was true for my friends in high school, as they were used by the boys they slept with, the pop culture that shaped them, and the Planned Parenthood clinic that provided their abortions for a few hundred bucks. And this was the case for myself and my college girlfriends, as we were easily used by a social movement, our allegiance purchased with a cheap and thoughtless *my body, my choice.*

Abortion is the deadliest empty promise of our age.

Just like the reckless living the Prodigal pursued in a far country, abortion promises life, satisfaction, and real fulfillment. Instead, it delivers death, regret, and myriad wounds, physical and otherwise.

May we all come to our senses and return to the Father's warm, forgiving, and enduring embrace. May we actively and persistently push back the culture of death in our midst. Our good God is a resurrection God. His specialty is bringing life from death. This is what he does! May he do it here and now. May we choose life.

Maybe you yourself had an abortion (or maybe more than one), or maybe you encouraged your friend or daughter to get one, or maybe you've just avoided the issue altogether and lulled yourself into complacency thinking this isn't your problem. Whatever role you have played in the counterfeit of abortion, know this: "There is therefore now no condemnation for those who are in Christ Jesus" (Rom. 8:1). Do not let the enemy steal the joy of your salvation, the lightheartedness of your freedom, the peace and hope you have for all eternity. He is not welcome here. You were made for so much more. Our God reigns.

Discussion Questions

1. Start with an awareness that one in four American women has an abortion. There are likely some women in your group who have

ABORTION HAS NOT DELIVERED

endured the trauma of abortion. Proceed through this discussion with care and concern for their perspective.

2. Whether it was for expediency or by design or subconsciously, the Sexual Revolution labeled the male body normal and made birth control for females. How might your life, your mother's life, or others' lives be different if, instead of suppressing pregnancy, we celebrated it? What if efforts used to create birth control and abortion were instead navigated toward creative means of adjusting both the public and private spheres for new life?

3. Fetuses were determined by the Supreme Court not to be persons back in 1973. Our culture says that to be a person one must be able to define oneself. How pervasive is this thinking? How dangerous is it? What do you think defines a person?

4. Under the section "Abortion: The Data" there are six subsections. Which data are the most surprising to you? Why do you think much of this research remains undisclosed or unpopular to the public?

5. Do you agree or disagree that we all bear the blame for abortion? What is your plan to help reduce the number of abortions in your community?

6. Many post-abortive women believe their abortions are unforgivable, but this is a lie. Read Psalm 104; Romans 8:1; 2 Corinthians 7:10; John 8:36; 14:19; and 1 John 1:9. Encourage one another with these truths of Scripture and close by praying and thanking God that he is relentlessly forgiving and can bring life from death.

7

Trending: LGBTQIA+

"FOUR YEARS AGO, married to the father of my three children, I fell in love with a woman." That's the first sentence of the first chapter in a *New York Times* bestseller, which is also, as of this writing, ranked number one on Amazon for Christian Self-Help. The book is *Untamed*, by Glennon Doyle, who, according to the publisher, *People* says "might just be the patron saint of female empowerment." It's Doyle's memoir and manifesto. It's the story of how she, and all women, are raised caged, but must set themselves free. It's the story of how to become untamed.

As a women's ministry leader, when a bestseller like this quotes the Bible and admonishes women, "Maybe Eve was never meant to be our warning. Maybe she was meant to be our model. Own your wanting. Eat the apple. Let it burn"—*and it's number one in Christian self-help*—I know I have to enter the conversation.[1]

Doyle's voice is loud and winsome, but it's just one of many. In the last couple of decades leaders and authors like her have

---

1 Glennon Doyle, *Untamed* (New York: The Dial Press, 2020), 122.

increased a hundredfold throughout society and inside the Christian church. They're well meaning. They seek to encourage. They say *love is love* and double down with *God is love*. They mean to lift up the marginalized, to protect the vulnerable. As the culture lurches left and celebrates all things LGBTQIA+, they want the church to be all-in too.

Their rhetoric is powerful and persuasive. We feel the cultural pressure, we see Christian leaders embracing it, and we wonder what we're supposed to do. It's a huge tension for all of us. I love God and I love his people, so I have a responsibility to go here. Trust me, I would much rather mind my own business and drink coffee on my couch with my yellow lab snoring beside me. If reading this chapter is uncomfortable for you, know that it was for me to write it too. It has been sown in tears and that deep-groaning kind of prayer.

What I long for you and me to know is that there is a better narrative. There is a better story. In a world that says the most important thing about you is whom you love (*identify the initial on the spectrum that feels right to you—this is who you are*), I want to push back and say no, that's a lie that leads to death. The most important thing about you is who loves you. And that's a truth that leads to everlasting life.

It's not *whom you love*; it's *who loves you* that is the real foundation for your life and mine.[2]

We are children of God (1 John 3:1). He is the author of our lives and the author of our faith. Standing on Christ alone, we can receive the truth that sets us free. The sexual ideologies of our age promise life but deliver death. You and I were made for so much more.

---

2 My thanks to Sam Allberry for sharing this truth in *Why Does God Care Who I Sleep With?* (Charlotte: The Good Book Company, 2020), 103, where he in turn credits Jojo Ruba for this insight.

But first, a caveat. The LGBTQIA+ spectrum, movement, and history are *vast*. LGBTQIA+ stands for lesbian, gay, bisexual, transgender, questioning or queer, intersex, ally or asexual, and the plus sign is an umbrella for the inclusion of anyone else on the sexual orientation or gender identity (SOGI) spectrum. A comprehensive discussion on sexual orientation and gender identity would require parsing out limitless and ever-evolving issues (things like the nature vs. nurture debate, changes in mental health diagnoses and treatments, the role of childhood influences and sexual abuse, the uniqueness of early onset disorders, the variations and reasons behind using words such as *lifestyle* or *choice* or *sin*, and I could go on). It is not the goal of this chapter to address all of the issues presented by the LGBTQIA+ spectrum.

The scope of this chapter is limited to a phenomenon that is unfolding across Western countries right now: more women and girls than ever before now say they identify as LGBT. The last decade alone has seen a sharp and unprecedented jump amongst, predominantly, girls and young women in the wealthy West. Maybe that's you, or maybe that's someone you love.

Readers of this chapter will likely fall into one of two categories. You might personally be struggling to understand your own SOGI identity, and I pray you will keep reading and reaching for an understanding of God's good design. I don't underestimate the burdens you bring to the table as you turn these pages. Or you might be reading as someone who has friends and family who seek their identity on the LGBTQIA+ spectrum. I pray you too will keep reading and reaching for an understanding of God's good design.

Whatever it is you are balancing as you read the pages ahead, my prayer is that you and I will interpret all of our identity questions and burdens through the lens of our unchanging and good Creator and Savior.

Trending Upward amongst Young Women and Girls

Let's start by taking a look at the data, because the population of adults who identify as LGBT is growing faster than ever. One in six Gen Z young adults identifies as LGBT, according to Gallup data from 2020. Amongst Gen Z who identify as LGBT, 72 percent said they identify as bisexual, which means almost 12 percent of all Gen Z adults identify as bisexual. By contrast, about half of millennials (the next generation older) who identify as LGBT, say they are bisexual.[3]

Of all American adults age eighteen and older, 5.6 percent identify as LGBT, which is up from 4.5 percent in Gallup's 2017 data. More than half of LGBT adults identify as bisexual, which means 3.1 percent of all American adults now identify as bisexual.

Women are more likely than men to identify as LGBT, and especially as bisexual. More than 4 percent of women identify as bisexual, and less than 2 percent of men do.[4] Research from the Williams Institute at the UCLA School of Law reveals that bisexual women make up the largest group of LGBT adults—about 35 percent.[5] Additionally, more than one in ten United States high school youth identifies as LGBTQ. Among them, 75 percent are female, and 77 percent identify as bisexual.[6]

---

3   Statistics in this paragraph and the following are from Jeffrey M. Jones, "LGBT Identification Rises to 5.6% in Latest U.S. Estimate," *Gallup*, February 24, 2021, https://news.gallup.com/.
4   Jones, "LGBT Identification Rises."
5   Samantha Schmidt, "1 in 6 Gen Z Adults Are LGBT. And This Number Could Continue to Grow," *The Washington Post*, February 24, 2021, https://www.washingtonpost.com/.
6   Schmidt, "1 in 6 Gen Z adults."

The main takeaway from all of this new data is that the LGBT population is increasing due to growth in younger generations, and the majority of that is happening amongst women and girls.

I have seen the above statistics play out in my own women's Bible studies and groups of friends. Eight to ten years ago, several friends who experienced same-sex attraction perceived it through a biblical lens. They shared their temptations with our church small groups, asked for accountability, and took the way of escape for years (1 Cor. 10:13). It was my honor to engage in the battle with them, pray with them, rehearse the truth with them, and be held up by them as well, as they battled my temptations with me.

But over time, they left the local church, the broader Christian church began to grant permission and even celebration of lesbianism, bisexuality, and transgenderism, and all of them have now surrendered. A decade ago they fought what they perceived to be ungodly and unbiblical temptations. Today they are in same-sex marriages, and one has transitioned to a man.

The wider cultural trend, reflected in growing numbers and an ever-increasing list of identity possibilities, is also very personal. I write with dearly loved names and faces in mind. Navigating this cultural trend with both grace and truth is not easy for any of us.

The Social Contagion and How It Spreads

Across Western nations over the last decade, there has been "a 1,000–5,000% increase in (mostly white) teenage females seeking treatment from gender clinics and psychologists."[7] Whereas "before 2012 there was no scientific literature on girls ages eleven to twenty-one ever

---

7   Preston Sprinkle, "Trans* Teenagers and Abigail Shrier's Irreversible Damage," *The Center for Faith, Sexuality & Gender* (blog), December 28, 2020, https://centerforfaith.com/.

having developed gender dysphoria at all,"[8] these girls now constitute the majority of those seeking treatment for gender dysphoria.

Abigail Shrier sounded the alarm when she released *Irreversible Damage: The Transgender Craze Seducing Our Daughters* in 2020. The book includes more than two hundred pages of statistics, interviews, and stories told by girls afflicted with Rapid Onset Gender Dysphoria (ROGD), their parents, transgender social media influencers, educators, therapists, and medical doctors.

ROGD, which is a new diagnosis, is not the same as traditional gender dysphoria, which is marked by persistent dysphoria from early childhood. ROGD is marked by a sudden onset in teens who have never before experienced discomfort with their gender, and it arises almost solely amongst socially connected groups of girls. The presence of a rapid onset, as well as the prevalence of ROGD amongst peer groups, indicates that ROGD is driven by a social contagion. This means that many researchers, practitioners, and parents alike suspect that the recent spikes in gender dysphoria— the uptick in the statistics covered in the previous section—are due primarily to the influence of one's friends. A similar contagious phenomenon has been seen amongst girls in recent history with anorexia and cutting.

The alarm sounded by Shrier focuses on how across-the-board a gender-affirming approach is taken by educators, therapists, doctors, and school counselors when a girl experiencing ROGD comes to them. The vast majority are trained to affirm a girl's self-diagnosis of gender dysphoria. There is little regard for other presenting mental health issues or typical teenage anxiety. As documented by interviews across the nation, parents are actively shut out and

---

8 Abigail Shrier, *Irreversible Damage: The Transgender Craze Seducing Our Daughters* (Washington, DC: Regnery Publishing, 2020), xxi.

permanent steps are often taken without much, if any, pause to change a girl's body and future forever. Shrier paints a concerning picture that a girl must only declare she's transgender, and all of the experts and professionals follow her lead.

The rise in ROGD is not surprising when we consider sweeping changes in education curricula, social media content, and cultural norms over the last few decades. Starting in kindergarten, many schools teach a sort of gender taxonomy (using, for example, the Genderbread Person or Gender Unicorn). The goal is to teach children that their identity, expression, sex, gender, and sexual orientation can all be different things—meaning, their bodies and minds are not unified. (Remember the dualism of body and mind we looked at in the last chapter?) Schools offer clubs, activities, and special days and months to recognize and celebrate children who identify as LGBTQIA+. Children pick their own pronouns, and oftentimes schools do not tell their parents if their pronouns do not match their biological sex, out of a concern that the children will be mistreated at home. Puberty blockers and social transitioning (behaving as the opposite sex) are seen as neutral first steps. College health plans offer cross-sex hormones and even gender-changing surgeries. Best practices amongst therapists, counselors, and doctors are only gender-affirming and follow the lead of the child. All the while, parents are told their daughters are likely to commit suicide if they don't fully cooperate.

Never mind the reality that 70 percent of children who experience gender dysphoria outgrow it.[9] Shrier interviewed numerous desisters (those who desist in their dysphoria and pursue a detransition). These young women say that transitioning as teens

---

9 Shrier, *Irreversible Damage*, 119.

gave them a way of escape from stress at home, anxiety at school, or whatever was pressuring them at the time. They watched social media influencers proclaim that testosterone saved them. When they posed the idea that they might be transgender to friends, teachers, or counselors, they were met only with unfettered positive reinforcement. *You're so brave! I'm so proud of you!* Therapists and doctors and gender clinics did all they could to be gender-affirming.

More than one desister said the world they inhabited was like a "cult." On the inside, one says, "you believe non-reality and you disbelieve reality." And there is a high price if one second-guesses her trans identity. Shaming is the "key mechanism for controlling the behavior of the suddenly trans-identified."[10]

The whole movement is, oddly, regressive. When educators, counselors, and influencers repeat, for example, that boys like blue and girls like pink, so if you're a girl who likes blue you must really be a boy, the movement erases diversity. Ironically, those who think they're the most progressive and freedom-seeking are, in fact, further binding boys and girls to limiting and untrue stereotypes.

Academicians, pediatricians, educators, and all of the West's most elite youth and sexuality practitioners are in deep. In their singular focus, they leave girls' other mental health issues untreated. I don't doubt their compassion and desire to serve children well, but they are doing exactly what Shrier's book title says: inflicting irreversible damage on an entire generation of hurting girls.

Confusing *How* We Are with *Who* We Are

In 2020 actress Ellen Page, the star of *The Umbrella Academy, Juno,* and the *X-Men* series, announced she would identify as

---

10 Quotations from Shrier, *Irreversible Damage,* 188–89.

a man and henceforth go by the name Elliot Page. While Page began his Twitter announcement with gratitude for others' support and elation at finally being his "authentic self," the bulk of the message has a threatening tone. "My joy is real, but it is also fragile," Page says, "I'm scared. . . . To [those who] spew hostility towards the trans community: you have blood on your hands . . . we won't be silent in the face of your attacks."[11] Becket Cook, author and Hollywood production designer, who was once a gay atheist but encountered Jesus Christ and is now celibate, says, "As much as Page's trans decision has been met with jubilant applause, the tone of his own announcement suggests his 'new self' is tenuous at best—alarmingly dependent on the affirmation and acceptance of others."[12]

When we declare that *how* we are is *who* we are, we do indeed become tenuous, fragile, and dependent. If my authentic self is that I am a Christian writer, then what happens to me if I succumb to sin in a way that disqualifies me from Christian ministry? Or what if I just don't want to write anymore? If what I *do* is who I *am*, then I must always perform, always behave just so, and relentlessly seek the approval of others to make sure I'm doing it right.

We humans are finite, frail, and fickle. We take on a role meant for God alone when we create our own identities and conjure up our own worth. We have to be our own god, our own source of meaning, our own source of power and reason for being. The truth

---

11 Elliot Page (@TheElliotPage), Twitter, December 1, 2020, 10:10 a.m., https://twitter.com /TheElliotPage/status/1333820783655837701?ref_src=twsrc%5Etfw%7Ctwcamp%5E tweetembed%7Ctwterm%5E1334195506696884228%7Ctwgr%5E%7Ctwcon%5Es3_ &ref_url=https%3A%2F%2Fwww.thegospelcoalition.org%2Farticle%2Fhollywood-elliot -page-me%2F.

12 Becket Cook, "Why Hollywood Praises Elliot Page (And Blacklists Me)," The Gospel Coalition, December 10, 2020, https://www.thegospelcoalition.org/.

is, we cannot bear up under that. Our identity and worth must come from a source outside of ourselves, bigger than ourselves, more permanent and stable than ourselves, better, more beautiful, and truer than ourselves. Our identity must be rooted in something (Someone) unchanging, immovable, and eternal.

Page is scared and angry because he knows his identity is dependent on the buy-in and affirmation of other finite, frail, and fickle humans. His existence is tenuous because it's self-reliant. Indeed, Page, now trans, was only just recently married to a woman, but divorced her after coming out as a man.

The truth is, he and all of us were made not to rely on ourselves or to determine ourselves, but to rest in our immutable, loving, and good Creator.

The Coup against Our Creator

Today in the West, we believe the most important thing about us is our sexual desire. Sex has become so central to our way of life that to deny others their sexual preference or their sexual ambitions is to deny them their own identity and their chance at happiness. We have so idolized romance and eroticism and relationships that to limit any of those expressions, we think, is to limit authenticity and life itself. Rehearsing a biblical sexual ethic is now considered hate speech across campuses, in newspapers, and in legislation.

Christopher Yuan is now an author and professor at Moody Bible Institute. But years ago, he says, "Sexuality was the core of who I was, and everything and everyone around me affirmed that. And if *I am gay* truly means that's *who I am*, it would be utterly cruel for someone to condemn me for simply being myself. Yet we know that we are created in God's image (Gen. 1:27). Thus, rejecting our inherent essence and replacing it simply with what we feel or do is in reality an attempted coup d'état against our Creator."[13]

We see here again dualistic thinking. Rather than seeing humans as unified, embodied souls, this way of thinking says "our true self is different than the body we live in . . . our body is something less than us, and can be used, shaped, and changed to match how we feel."[14]

But is there any other sphere outside of gender and sexuality where we say what we *feel* trumps who we really *are*?

What if a black teenage girl goes to her counselor and says, "I feel white"? What if the counselor encourages the girl to go by a culturally accepted white name, engage in white activities, and seek out treatment to change the color of her skin and the texture of her hair? The counselor would rightly be fired and her license revoked, and there would be an appropriate public outcry. Rather, the ethical course of action would be for the counselor to help the girl see that her black skin and hair are beautiful, that her life as a black girl is important and infinitely worthy, that the world needs her good contribution as the black girl she was created to be.

Likewise, we don't say to a girl who is dangerously thin but only sees obesity when she looks in the mirror, "Yes, because you feel overweight, you must really be." The proper course of treatment for a girl with a body dysmorphic disorder is to help her feel comfortable in her body, to help her treat her body with respect and healthy practices, and to match her feelings about her body to what's true about her body.

---

13 Christopher Yuan, *Holy Sexuality and the Gospel: Sex, Desire, and Relationships Shaped by God's Grand Story* (Colorado Springs: Multnomah, 2016), 9–10.

14 Andrew Walker, *God and the Transgender Debate: What Does the Bible Actually Say about Gender Identity?* (Charlotte, NC: The Good Book Company, 2018), 26.

As we've said already, the female body is glorious and good and worth protecting and cherishing. The female body is not broken. Female physiology does not need to be fixed. Decades from now I fear a similar outcome to that of abortion: millions will be disfigured or dead, and we will realize that the irreversible damage never had to be. We will see that a more integral and body-unifying approach to supporting suffering girls would have been far better.

Did God Really Say That?

We are creatures with a Creator. We have a God who made us and knows what's best for us. We know *who* we are because we know *whose* we are. For Christians, our Creator is also our Savior. Not only did he make us, but he died on the cross to save us.

Rachel Gilson, a theologian who serves in college ministry, authored *Born This Way*, her own story of coming out as a lesbian, then coming to faith, and then aligning her life with Jesus. She says, "The language [of the gospel] is so immersive: if by faith we receive his righteousness, we enter *in* to Christ (Gal. 3:26). We are literally owned by him. We don't own us; our friends don't own us; our families don't own us; our attractions don't own us. Only Jesus owns us."[15]

This is the better story—we belong to Jesus. It is he who loves us, and that's the most important thing about us.

We need only to remember the cross to know that Jesus is infinitely good, merciful, and trustworthy. It is in our own best interest to trust him, walk with him, and honor him. He doesn't need our obedience; we do.

---

15 Rachel Gilson, *Born Again This Way: Coming Out, Coming to Faith, and What Comes Next* (Charlotte, NC: The Good Book Company, 2020), 133.

What follows is just a sampling of what the Bible says about gender identity, sexual orientation, sexuality, and relationships. This is by no means an exhaustive list of what can be found in Scripture, but these truths are persistently helpful to me, as I seek to navigate the empty promises of our age for myself and with others.

To express his image God created both male and female. The creation of both male and female was neither accidental nor an afterthought (Gen. 1:27). The two genders are by design and needed. Gilson points out, "Sex difference is a key way that God's image is displayed in humanity."[16]

Both genders are necessary to create new life. God called Adam and Eve to be fruitful and multiply (Gen. 1:28). Both men and women are privileged to be subcreators. The physical form of each gender makes it obvious that they belong to one another; their unique parts create a whole. In fact, the union of both fleshes is actually a *reunion*, as Eve was brought out of Adam (Gen. 2:21), and then in sexual union they are put back together again.

Jesus confirms the Genesis blueprint. Jesus affirmed the truth and implications of creation when the Pharisees tested him about divorce. He said, "Have you not read that he who created them from the beginning made them male and female, and said, 'Therefore a man shall leave his father and his mother and hold fast to his wife, and the two shall become one flesh'? So they are no longer two but one flesh. What therefore God has joined together, let not man separate" (Matt. 19:4–6). Jesus confirms that God created people; he created them male and female; only men and women can join in full sexual union with the opposite gender; and what God does, people should not undo.[17]

16 Gilson, *Born Again This Way*, 32.
17 Walker, *God and the Transgender Debate*, 59.

When humanity insists, God will give us over to our idolatry, to our lusts, to our dishonorable passions, and, ultimately, to death. Romans 1:21–31 are sobering verses, both for the first century and the twenty-first century. The verses clearly forbid exchanging natural relations *between* the genders for passion *within* the genders. Scripture is clear that "homosexual behavior is a sin, not according to who practices it or by what motivation they seek it, but because that act itself, as a truth-suppressing exchange, is contrary to God's good design."[18]

It is wrong to approve of sexual sin. Those who know God's righteous decrees but reject them, Paul says in Romans 1:32, deserve to die. This is a hard word for us, as we live in an age of "you do you." But we must remember we are fallen people and God is infinitely holy. The wages of our sin is death, but God stands ready to offer eternal life to those who will turn to him (Rom. 6:23).

The body is not meant for sexual immorality, but for the Lord, and the Lord for the body (1 Cor. 6:12–20). We are made by Jesus and for Jesus. Sexual sin is a wrong committed against our own bodies, the bodies of others, and against the Lord. Rather than asking, "What can I get away with?" we should ask instead, "How can I most honor God?"

Real Truth, Real Grace

Faithful followers of Jesus must make a difficult but necessary decision as to who they will follow: the strong cultural current of our day or the risen Jesus. I feel this deeply and personally. Even if I were to walk in perfect love toward the dear ones in my life who have embraced lesbianism and transgenderism, they know my views, and that alone can cause alienation and distance. And

18 Kevin DeYoung, *What Does the Bible Really Teach about Homosexuality?* (Wheaton: Crossway, 2015), 53.

of course, I don't walk in perfect love. I fall woefully short of the patience, gentleness, and compassion exhibited by my Savior toward me and toward them. My prayer and desire is to love them with both grace and truth, and to entrust them to our good God.

The word of God is full of hard truths, especially when it comes to gender and sexuality in our day. May it be the word of God that offends and not our own pride, arrogance, or unkindness. We may *sound* like bigots, because we hold to a biblical sexual ethic that has been rejected and mocked, but let's not actually *be* bigots. We are saved by grace through faith; it is not our own doing (Eph. 2:8–9). Therefore, there should never be even a whiff of pride or arrogance in our own behaviors. Apart from Christ we are nothing. Apart from the saving work of Jesus, we are damned.

So then, let us not demonize same-sex attraction or transgenderism or anything else on the LGBTQIA+ spectrum as a special class of ugly or unforgivable sins. To classify homosexual sin as worse than heterosexual sin is to grant those who are not same-sex-attracted unmerited self-righteousness. It also weakens our response to other sexual sins like pornography, adultery, or sexual abuse—categorizing those as somehow less of an affront to our holy God.

I like Christopher Yuan's suggestion: "Instead of differentiating between opposite-sex desires and same-sex desires, let's use the biblical categories of good desires and sinful desires."[19] We must *all* repent of sexual sin and walk in dependence on our good God.

Take the Way of Escape

Andrew Walker, author of *God and the Transgender Debate*, says it's important that we distinguish between experiencing a feeling and

---

19 Yuan, *Holy Sexuality*, 69.

acting on a feeling. He says, "Individuals who experience gender dysphoria are not sinning when such experiences occur. To feel that your body is one sex and your self is a different gender is not sinful. . . . This experience is a sign that all of our selves are as broken by sin as the creation around us is."[20] And temptation is not a sin, as even Jesus experienced temptation (Heb. 4:15). Even as we follow our Lord, we will experience temptation until we reach heaven.

The question is, How will we choose to respond to dysphoria and temptation? Paul says, "God is faithful, and he will not let you be tempted beyond your ability, but with the temptation he will also provide the way of escape, that you may be able to endure it" (1 Cor. 10:13). Temptation is not sin, but it is not to be taken lightly. We must grab hold of the way out when unbiblical desires arise. Walker concludes, "Deciding to let [a dysphoric] feeling rule—to feed that feeling so that it becomes the way you see yourself and the way you identify yourself and the way you act—is sinful, because it is deciding that your feelings will have authority over you, and will define what is right and what is wrong."[21]

There is not sufficient space here to carefully delineate the differences and commonalities between temptations and dysphoria. And there is not space to consider the sins that are committed against us and what role those play in our acting out sexual sins as a result (i.e., sexual assault and abuse against children). What I want to make clear here is that those who find themselves either tempted or dysphoric should feel neither shame nor condemnation, but rather recognize that temptations are deeply antagonistic. Urgently take the way out and seek the care and accountability of a local church, as well as a licensed Christ-honoring counselor.

20 Walker, *God and the Transgender Debate*, 68.
21 Walker, *God and the Transgender Debate*, 68.

The bottom line is that continued sin hardens the heart, but repentance restores to us the joy of our salvation (Ps. 51:12).

Do Not Hang a Millstone

I have to remind myself every day that sin and Christ cannot abide together. He calls us to come and die, that we might be born again, in him. The words of the gospel are certain and violent: "Put to death therefore what is earthly in you" (Col. 3:5); put on holiness (3:12); and "whatever you do, in word or deed, do everything in the name of the Lord Jesus" (3:17).

Christians are sinners who are daily being renewed from the inside out. Christians look to the cross and remember that we have been bought with the blood of Jesus. He is worthy of our obedience. Our sin and his Spirit cannot remain together within us. "Those who belong to Christ Jesus have crucified the flesh with its passion and desires" (Gal. 5:24).

Rosaria Butterfield, who writes about her conversion to Christ and departure from lesbianism in *The Secret Thoughts of an Unlikely Convert*, says that when leaders in the church say you can keep your indwelling sin and have everlasting life too, they hang a millstone around the necks of those who might surrender fully to Jesus.[22] They elevate their own views and the world's views above God's truth. In their rejection or rewriting of Scripture, they think they are more merciful than the God who endured the cross to save us.

But so much is at stake. Real image-bearing souls, everlasting life, sanctification, and true deep-down happiness in Jesus all hang in the balance. Christ-followers are commanded to have mercy and save

---

22 Many thanks to Rosaria Butterfield for proclaiming this truth in *Love Your Neighbor Enough to Speak Truth*, The Gospel Coalition, October 31, 2016, https://www.thegospelcoalition.org/.

others by snatching those who doubt out of the fire (Jude 22–23). We can entrust our dear ones and ourselves to Jesus. For the joy set before him, Jesus endured the cross (Heb. 12:2).

Whether our cross is speaking grace and truth at a great cost, or it's leaving a life of sexual sin for the joy set before us, with God's help we can endure it.

Yes, God really did say all of that. The empty promises of our age deliver death because they contradict the giver of life. Jesus offers true, everlasting, abundant life when we die to ourselves and live again in him. There really is nothing better.

A People Set Apart

God's call on us is to be holy, not heterosexual. The object of the gospel is not our behavior but our hearts. As Jackie Hill Perry says in her book *Gay Girl, Good God*, "God was not calling me to be straight; He was calling me to Himself."[23] In holiness, not heterosexuality, there is real, soul-deep freedom. In surrendering to the mercy and love of our Savior, there is freedom. Jesus came that we may have abundant life, real life, full life (John 10:10). This is the best news!

This chapter (and this book) is not a message of *be good girls and behave*; it's a pleading to embrace your good God so that you might taste and possess real freedom. Freedom is not the absence of restrictions. Freedom is knowing your nature and thriving in the way you were designed.

Here's an overused but helpful illustration: a fish is not free outside of his bowl of water. He was designed for the water, and it's for his good to stay immersed. To reject his design is to his demise. Our design is to be reconciled to our God.

---

23 Jackie Hill Perry, *Gay Girl, Good God: The Story of Who I Was and Who God Has Always Been* (Nashville: B&H, 2018), 69.

Glennon Doyle's inspiration for *Untamed* came when she saw a cheetah at the zoo and felt compassion on the creature because she was caged, when she was designed to run free across the African plain. Doyle translated that experience to herself, equating the cheetah's cage with society's expectations on her as a woman. She wanted the cheetah to be free, and she wanted herself to be free. But just as surely as the cheetah was designed to run free, Glennon Doyle was designed in the image of God, to be a woman who has "natural relations" with a man, not "those that are contrary to nature" with another woman (Rom. 1:26). Doyle traded the cage of society's expectations for the cage of lesbianism. Neither the cultural expectations she wanted to throw off nor homosexuality reflect her true nature.

Our true nature is to worship our King. We were made by God and for God (Col. 1:16). We were made to be a people set apart, "a chosen race, a royal priesthood, a holy nation, a people for his own possession, that [we] may proclaim the excellencies of him who called [us] out of darkness into his marvelous light" (1 Pet. 2:9).

You and I were made for Jesus. *Who loves us* is far more important than *whom we love.*

The truth of *who* loves us changes us. God conforms those he loves into the image of his Son (Rom. 8:29). We become more and more like Jesus every day (2 Cor. 3:18). And as we love God, we want to keep his commands (John 14:15). Holiness leads to obedience. God's commands set us free.

True freedom is in coming home. True freedom is running into the arms of our Father and receiving and wearing the best robe, his ring on our hand, his shoes on our feet (Luke 15:22). True freedom is feasting and eating and celebrating with our God (Luke 15:23). True freedom is in being found when we were lost, in being made alive again when we were dead (Luke 15:24).

Come, let's celebrate the best story. We've been invited in.

Discussion Questions

1. What's your personal perception of or experience with authors and leaders who celebrate the LGBTQIA+ spectrum, both inside and outside the church? Are their books and ideas popular in your sphere? Do you feel like your church community leans toward affirming or condemning or seeking a biblical ethic of grace and truth when it comes to these issues?

2. Have you witnessed the social contagion of women and girls increasingly identifying as transgender or gay in your own community? How is your community responding well or poorly?

3. Discuss this statement: When we declare that *how* we are is *who* we are, we do indeed become tenuous, fragile, and dependent. In this chapter we saw an example of that with Elliot Page, and I also shared an example from my own life as a Christian writer. What's an area where you are tempted to think *who* you are is *how* you are?

4. Under the section titled "Did God Really Say That?" there are seven biblical principles for looking at gender and sexuality issues. Which one is most helpful to you? Or new to you? Or hard for you?

5. Read Romans 1:18–32 and 1 Corinthians 6:12–20. Jackie Hill Perry says, "God was not calling me to be straight; He was calling me to Himself." That's true for everyone. It's what Christopher Yuan calls *Holy Sexuality*. Faithful followers of Jesus must make a difficult but necessary decision as to whom they will follow: the

strong cultural current of our day or the risen Jesus. What might that look like in your own life?

6. What do you think about the truth that it's not *whom you love* but it's *who loves you* that really matters? Close by reading and praying John 14:15–17, thanking the Holy Spirit for his help and asking him to enable you to obey the Father.

8

When Marriage and Motherhood Become Idols

"MOTHERHOOD IS A WOMAN'S HIGHEST CALLING." It was said with awe, reverence, and authority. And it was said at a baby shower I went to a couple years ago. I was in attendance along with various friends, including one deeply saddened by infertility and one who longed to be married.

Knowing my friends' burdens, the statement stung like a slap on the cheek. I inwardly debated whether or not to stand up right then and there and say, "Sorry, that's absolutely not true." If you've ever led a Bible study or hosted more than a few people with more than a few opinions, you know the feeling. Say something now for the sake of everyone in the room, or let it go and try to do damage control later?

I went with the latter option, not having it in me at the time to sour the mood of the shower. I called my friend facing infertility as soon as I got in my car to go home. "I am so sorry you had to hear that," I said. She's smart and strong in the Lord and took it in stride, but it had left a mark for sure. We lamented the destructive impact the falsity might have had on everyone else in the room. My other friend, the single one in attendance, was unphased, her eye still on the prize of assumed marriage and motherhood in her future.

Really? Idols?

We love a story that ends with true love and happily ever after. We're raised on fairy tales: the sweet couple overcoming all odds, uniting in the end, and raising beautiful children while the sun sets in the distance. It's the stuff of romantic comedies, Hallmark movies, and almost every Disney story.

First comes love, then comes marriage, then comes the baby in the baby carriage.

And indeed, marriage and motherhood are good gifts. You will never catch me saying otherwise. Romantic love is a blessing. Covenantal love in marriage is remarkable. Marriage as a symbol of Christ's love for the church (as discussed in chap. 5) induces awe and worship in me. Children are a gift from the Lord (Ps. 127:3). Whoever receives these gifts should rejoice and steward them well.

But the Christian church—at least the church in the United States, which I love and serve with my whole heart—has a tendency to set marriage and motherhood on a pedestal that Scripture does not support. Remember, "an idol is whatever you look at and say, in your heart of hearts, 'If I have that, then I'll feel my life has meaning, then I'll know I have value, then I'll feel significant and secure.'"[1]

Idols are good things that we turn into ultimate things.

1 Timothy Keller, *Counterfeit Gods: The Empty Promises of Money, Sex, and Power, and the Only Hope That Matters* (New York: Dutton, 2009), xviii.

Church Chatter

We in the church can know we've made marriage and motherhood idols by the way we talk about them and frame them in our ministries and programs. Our words and church bulletins reveal, even though it's likely subconscious, that we can't imagine that unmarried or childless adults have really "arrived." We doubt their maturity until they have a spouse and some kids to prove it.

I know many singles and childless couples who have been wounded, confused, or angered by thoughtless comments made by members of their church family:

- Are you dating anyone? I know someone I can fix you up with.
- Don't worry; you'll find the right person soon.
- The *real* sanctification happens when you get married (or have kids).
- You wouldn't know; you're not a mom (or dad) yet.

Single and childless adults often feel they're an afterthought. They know they're usually the last ones to be considered to host or lead an event. They sense that others think they're living a prolonged adolescence. And so, many simply leave the church. A recent LifeWay study reveals that amongst Christians ages twenty-three to thirty who stopped regularly attending church, 29 percent said it was because they no longer felt connected to the people there.[2]

---

2 Aaron Earls, "Most Teenagers Drop Out of Church as Young Adults," *LifeWay Research*, January 15, 2019, https://lifewayresearch.com.

Trying to Counter the Culture

Marriage and motherhood are good gifts, and they might feel out of place in a book about cultural counterfeits. But, like all good gifts, if we look to marriage and motherhood for our ultimate meaning, value, significance, or security, rather than to God himself, then they do indeed become idols. We, especially in the church, can place more weight on these temporary and secondary gifts than they are meant to bear. But how did that happen? How did we come to do this?

For decades the church has been busy fighting cultural counterfeits that are basically the exact opposite of marriage and motherhood—things already mentioned in this book, like the autonomy of self, hooking up, and abortion. The church has been right to react against the ways the Sexual Revolution has denigrated women, marriage, and families. But in so doing, we have unwittingly devalued singleness and childlessness, which are no less valuable, no less designed by God, and no less intended by our Creator than marriage and parenthood.

Author Rebecca McLaughlin concludes, "While we are right to champion marriage above any other form of sexual relationship (from promiscuity on the one hand to long–term cohabitation on the other), we are not right to champion marriage above faithful singleness. The apostle Paul would not be impressed."[3]

Seeds Sown in Purity Culture

My family once attended a wedding where the bride's purity took center stage. Several times during the ceremony the pastor men-

---

3 Rebecca McLaughlin (@RebeccMcLaugh), Twitter, April 29, 2020, 9:22 a.m., https://twitter .com/RebeccMcLaugh/status/1255517844751691776.

tioned her purity. It was celebrated in every speech during the reception, and it was also lauded in our conversations with various family members of the bridal party. On the one hand, it was beneficial to consider and publicly rejoice over a countercultural commitment to abstain from sex until marriage. On the other hand, it was, well, really weird. The centering of the bride, rather than both members of the couple and rather than Jesus, just felt *off*.

Neither my husband nor I grew up entrenched in Christian church culture. While we sometimes grieve that our childhoods lacked deep church community, we also know it was God's good plan for us. In fact, there are now a few things that we can look back on and be grateful that we missed. One of those things is the unforeseen damage caused by the purity movement of the late 1980s, 1990s, and early 2000s. Don't get me wrong; purity is good, and I think the church had good intentions with the purity movement. But on this side of it, we have to be honest and acknowledge the self-righteous moralism that it bred.

The evangelical Christian purity movement was marked by rallies, pledges, concerts, and ring ceremonies wherein Christian teens would promise to abstain from sex until marriage. In *Talking Back to Purity Culture*, Rachel Welcher describes how the purity movement fell in line with American individualism, teaching teens that making the personal decision to abstain from sex until marriage would benefit their lives, their marriages, their future families, and their reputations.[4] She says the movement "promised that premarital purity would result in a flourishing marriage. They told me that sexual obedience would secure a specific blessing."[5]

4   Rachel Welcher, *Talking Back to Purity Culture: Rediscovering Faithful Christian Sexuality* (Downers Grove: InterVarsity Press, 2020), 23.
5   Welcher, *Talking Back*, 7.

In this way, marriage, sex, and parenthood were shaped into a message of prosperity: *Do this to get that.* Or, more accurately, *Don't do this to get that.* Our moralistic behavior, it was taught, would deliver us our future. This is a false gospel. This is a lie that steals glory from Jesus. "Virginity does not provide our purity. Jesus does."[6]

The Older Brother

Much of Generation X and many Millennials grew up hearing this works-righteousness message. The result is nothing short of tragic: a relationship with God and living for his glory were traded in for the lesser gods of a good marriage, great sex, and great kids. Many put their hope in the empty promise of purity, instead of embracing the goodness of their God.

If the first four idols described in this book can be assigned to the Prodigal Son, then this one can be assigned to his older brother. When Jesus told the story of the prodigal son (Luke 15:11–32), he intended it for the ears of the Pharisees, who believed that blessing and salvation came through obedience to the Scriptures. Tim Keller says that the whole parable reveals that *both* self-discovery (the licentiousness of the younger brother) and moral conformity (the legalism of the older brother) prevent us from finding happiness and fulfillment in a relationship with the Father who made us.[7]

When the older brother finds out that his brother's reckless living has been rewarded with lavish gifts and a feast, he cries out in anger against his father, "Look, these many years I have served you, and I never disobeyed your command, yet you never gave me a young

6 Welcher, *Talking Back,* 29.
7 Timothy Keller, *Prodigal God: Recovering the Heart of the Christian Faith* (New York: Dutton, 2008), 29.

goat, that I might celebrate with my friends. But when this son of yours came, who has devoured your property with prostitutes, you kill the fattened calf for him!" (Luke 15:29–30).

Whereas the younger brother's reckless living distanced him from his father, in the case of the older brother it was his pride in his own moralistic behavior. The younger brother sought the good life in taking the father's wealth and setting out for the far country. The older brother sought the good life by earning the father's wealth through strict obedience. *Both sons* were after the father's riches, but not a relationship with the father himself.

For decades now the Christian church in the United States has witnessed the reckless living of the younger brother, as presented by the Sexual Revolution—exploiting bodies, cheap sex, pornography, divorce, homosexuality, abortion, and on and on—and set out to be, instead, the very good older brother. *We don't want to be like that*, we responded. *We will be pure, we will be good, we will be different.* And so, marriage and motherhood came to be exalted, idols on pedestals, two good gifts viewed as the best gifts, rewards for good behavior and making right choices.

An obvious problem, though, is that women who are not married or are not mothers are deemed lesser Christians. When we say "motherhood is a woman's highest calling," we are saying *out loud* that there is something wrong with you if you're not a mom. We are saying single and childless women don't measure up. We are saying they have not achieved God's *real* purpose for them.

Celibacy and Jesus

As we have seen in prior chapters, the Bible teaches that sexual union is designed for marriage between one man and one woman. Therefore, the only option for someone who is unmarried and committed to following the teachings of the Bible is celibacy. But celibacy seems absurd and fanatical to our Western minds.

Our immediate "Are you dating anyone?" or "Don't worry; you'll find someone soon" betray us. We in the church cannot fathom celibacy. To be single is to be lonely, we think; it is to lack intimacy.

But, as Sam Allberry wisely points out, to say that "a life without sexual fulfillment is not really an authentic way to live is actually saying that Jesus did not fully come in the flesh, that his was not a full human life. To say that it is dehumanizing to be celibate is to dehumanize Christ."[8]

The views we ingest and live by have real implications. Jesus was fully man, lived a worthy and full life, and was fully celibate. Celibacy, then, especially amongst Christ-followers, should not be seen as far-out and crazy, but rather as a good gift, worthy of our pursuit.

Receive It If You Can

Regarding singleness Jesus concluded, "Let the one who is able to receive this receive it" (Matt. 19:12). He said this after the Pharisees questioned him about marriage, and he cautioned them that what God has joined together man should not separate. They pressed him and pointed out that even Moses allowed certificates of divorce. Jesus replied, "Because of your hardness of heart Moses allowed you to divorce your wives, but from the beginning it was not so. And I say to you: whoever divorces his wife, except for sexual immorality, and marries another, commits adultery" (Matt. 19:8–9).

The disciples' response cracks me up: "If such is the case of a man with his wife, it is better not to marry" (Matt. 19:10). Can't

---

8 Sam Allberry, *7 Myths about Singleness* (Wheaton: Crossway, 2019), 26.

you just picture them? They probably looked at one another with raised eyebrows, thinking, *Whoa, you can never leave her? You can't marry anyone else? Better not to marry in the first place.*

Jesus went on to explain that there are eunuchs who have been so since birth, eunuchs made so by other men, and eunuchs who chose to be so for the sake of the kingdom of heaven (Matt. 19:11–12). Eunuchs were single and celibate men—some voluntarily choosing a life of abstinence in service to a ruler, and some involuntarily either by birth or castration. Either way, they received the gift of singleness. Jesus's use of eunuchs in this story "meant more than someone simply not marrying but rather one's setting aside the right of marriage and procreation. . . . Jesus is suggesting that there are some who will willingly give up the blessings of both marriage and offspring for sake of the kingdom of God."[9]

Jesus's bottom line was *receive singleness if you can.* It's a worthy and God-honoring endeavor to forgo a spouse and children for his sake.

The apostle Paul, also single, echoed the words of Jesus. He said, "Now as a concession, not a command, I say this. I wish that all were as I myself am. But each has his own gift from God, one of one kind and one of another. To the unmarried and the widows I say that it is good for them to remain single, as I am" (1 Cor. 7:6–8).

While marriage is certainly a gift, Paul is quick to remind us that singleness is too. A married man must be "anxious about worldly things, how to please his wife," and a married woman too "is anxious about worldly things, how to please her husband" (1 Cor. 7:33–34). That's the nature of marriage—you must be attentive

9 Barry Danylak, *Redeeming Singleness: How the Storyline of Scripture Affirms the Single Life* (Wheaton: Crossway, 2010), 153.

to the other's needs and desires. You must even be ready to forsake your own perceived calling in the interest of your spouse. I know so many couples where one spouse felt called to overseas missions but had to lay that dream down because the other spouse did not. This is what Paul is talking about. In marriage there are myriad concerns and considerations that simply do not apply when you are single.

The most highly acclaimed missionary ever and an author of much of the New Testament was inspired by the Holy Spirit to say he wishes all were single as he is. Why then do we insist that marriage is better?

Single or married, God has gifted you with your current state. God is sovereign, good, and trustworthy. He has not made a mistake. He has not forgotten you. He has ordained your marital status for his good purposes. I appreciate Allberry's conclusion: "If we balk at the idea of singleness being a gift, it is not because God has not understood us but because we have not understood him."[10]

Two Covenants and a Commission

Put your theology thinking cap on, and let's take a quick look at the two covenants and a commission that make up the storyline of the whole Bible. In Genesis 15 God made a covenant with Abraham and said, "'Look toward heaven, and number the stars, if you are able to number them.' Then he said to him, 'So shall your offspring be'" (Gen. 15:5). God was indicating that Abraham would father many nations and have children more numerous than the stars, and that they would be God's people.

We see the crowning of the new covenant in Jesus's last words, after his resurrection and before his ascension into heaven, when

---

10 Allberry, *7 Myths*, 37.

he gives his followers the Great Commission: "Go therefore and make disciples of all nations, baptizing them in the name of the Father and of the Son and of the Holy Spirit, teaching them to observe all that I have commanded you. And behold, I am with you always, to the end of the age" (Matt. 28:19–20).

God's family now grows as we share the gospel with others. The new covenant through Jesus fulfills God's covenant to Abraham. We are becoming more numerous than the stars in heaven, we are the offspring of Abraham as well as Jesus. We, the church, are the new Israel.

The Gospel Is Written in Jesus's Family Status

Every so often a documentary pops up on the History Channel claiming to have found an ancient text or artifact that proves Jesus had a secret wife and secret children. The documentaries, while fantastical and ever so popular, are always easily debunked by serious scholars. They only live on in grocery store paperbacks. If I'm honest, I've always considered Jesus's singleness and lack of biological children of no consequence. A sort of ho-hum, *that's what God wanted, I guess.*

But what I have come to understand and appreciate is that Jesus's singleness and lack of physical children is *central* to the gospel message.

Jesus's marital and family status was not simply a random circumstance, but rather by design and rich with meaning. First, "his singleness on earth bore witness to [the] ultimate marriage he came to establish."[11] As we saw in chapter 5, we will not be married to our earthly spouses in heaven, because all of us who are in Christ

11 Allberry, *7 Myths*, 120.

Jesus will be his bride and he will be our groom. I realize this is just as hard to understand in chapter 8 as it was back in chapter 5, but Jesus's unmarried status on earth points to the future reality that he is the groom and we, the church, are his bride.

Second, Jesus's lack of physical children is a bright reminder that we who follow him are his family. During his ministry on earth a crowd said to Jesus, "'Your mother and your brothers are standing outside, desiring to see you.' But he answered them, 'My mother and my brothers are those who hear the word of God and do it'" (Luke 8:20–21). Jesus shows us that the family of God is eternal and primary, while our nuclear families on earth are only temporary and secondary.

Spiritual ties bind stronger than biological ones.

Jesus, with his lavish love, promises that our spiritual families will be a hundred times more nourishing to us than our earthly moms, dads, siblings, spouses, and children. When Peter said to Jesus, "See, we have left our homes and followed you," Jesus replied, "There is no one who has left house or wife or brothers or parents or children, for the sake of the kingdom of God, who will not receive many times more in this time, and in the age to come eternal life" (Luke 18:28–30). While it's true that our God asks us to leave everything to follow him, he answers that sacrifice with the gift of himself, eternal life, and a family that spans all generations as well as the whole globe.

Christian, you and I belong to God. Our Father is God Almighty, Maker of heaven and earth. We are dearly loved. Our relationships with one another "are more permanent, and more precious, than relationships in [our physical] families."[12]

12 John Piper, "Single in Christ: A Name Better Than Sons and Daughters," *desiringGod.org*, April 29, 2007, https://www.desiringgod.org.

Family by Seclusion or Inclusion

What a different vision of family Jesus has for us than we typically see in Western life. In the day-to-day activities of the American nuclear family, Mom and Dad must be breadwinner, caregiver, lunch maker, sports coach, hobby teacher, vacation planner, family worship leader, and party thrower, not to mention disciplinarian, mentor, sage guide, and friend to their children. Allberry says, "People simply assume these family units are meant to be self-contained and self-sufficient. The aspiration is to have a wife or a husband, 2.5 children, a black Labrador, and a nice house. Once all this is acquired, you have what you need for doing life, so you then pull up the drawbridge and live happily ever after."[13]

My daughters were babies and little girls when we lived in Japan, and they ranged from kindergarten to high school when we lived in the Czech Republic. Our call to overseas missions left us with no other option than to embrace the family of God in our daily lives. My girls were immeasurably blessed by single women and childless married women who taught them piano, ballet, and art. They called women of no blood relation "aunt." They had big brothers and uncles who pushed them on the swing and shot hoops with them in our backyard. They really did have one hundred times the family, love, and gifts than my husband and I could have ever offered them on our own. Now that we're back in the States, this kind of daily living with others is much harder to come by. I must admit, we've given in somewhat to the pace of life here, the expectations for activities and pursuits. It's regrettable, really. Living at the pace of the American dream is not nearly as sweet as time spent just hanging out with our siblings in Christ.

13 Allberry, *7 Myths*, 70.

In an effort to push back against the cultural tide that seeks to dissolve the family, the church in the West has, in many ways, made the nuclear family ultimate. We worship our families when we make them central to our lives and identities. In stark contrast, here is what the Lord said to the eunuchs through the prophet Isaiah:

> To the eunuchs who keep my Sabbaths,
>> who choose the things that please me
>> and hold fast my covenant,
> I will give in my house and within my walls
>> a monument and a name
>> *better than sons and daughters*;
> I will give them an everlasting name
>> that shall not be cut off. (Isa. 56:4–5)

God says those who remain single and childless but hold fast to his covenant and keep his Sabbath—meaning those who obey him and trust him, those who rest in him—will receive blessings even better than sons and daughters. It is better to be in God's eternal family and be a member of his household than to have your own children. How different are these biblical truths than the ones we so often hear in Christian settings today. It's certainly a far cry from what I heard at that baby shower!

Let's Not Moralize Marriage and Motherhood

The thing about "motherhood is a woman's highest calling" is that it's a moral judgment. It says good women are moms. It says motherhood is the *best* way to be a female. I love being a mom and I count it one of my greatest joys, but it is by no means the result of my good behavior or my wise choices or an indication of my preferred status in God's kingdom. It is not who I am.

When we moralize marriage and motherhood in this way, we inadvertently create a hierarchy in the church with the moms on top (the more children the godlier) and the singles without children on the bottom. Unknowingly, we laud the former and alienate the latter.

Not only that, but we diminish diversity. My single friend who is a missionary and a spiritual mother to many says this false idea about motherhood reduces women to one dimension, when we are really made for so much more. Our God is creative and has designed each one of us with various skills, abilities, and resources. Whatever you and I do, in word or deed, let's do everything in the name of the Lord Jesus, giving thanks to God the Father through him (Col. 3:17).

For many of us, by God's grace that will be marriage and motherhood. For many of us, also by God's grace, that will be singleness and childlessness. Who knows what God has for each one of us?

Your highest calling and mine is not limited to a temporary role here on earth. Marriage and motherhood are fleeting. They cannot deliver the soul satisfaction we long for. Our spouses and children will falter and fail; they will never give us what only Jesus can, because you and I were created by Jesus and for Jesus.

If you have made marriage and motherhood the prize of your life—whether they are your roles now or you long for them to be—you will undoubtedly come up against anger and disappointment, because they will inevitably fall, as idols do. The older brother yells at his father, "Look, these many years I have served you, and I never disobeyed your command, yet you never gave me a young goat, that I might celebrate with my friends"

(Luke 15:29). He was after his father's goods, rather than the father himself. But just as the father went to the Prodigal, so our Father comes to us.

"Son," the father says, "you are always with me, and all that is mine is yours" (Luke 15:31). This promise is for you and me too. All that is the Father's is ours. He's been here with us all along, but we have not drawn near. We have sought the gifts instead of the giver. May it not be so. May you and I and every woman—married or not, childless or not—seek the things that are above, where Christ is. He is our life, and one day we will appear with him and his whole family in glory (Col. 3:2–4).

Discussion Questions

1. Have you heard someone say, "Motherhood is a women's highest calling"? Or have you ever heard other statements in Christian settings that inadvertently cause harm such as "Real sanctification happens when you get married" or "You wouldn't know; you're not a mom yet"? If statements like these have not been personally hard for you to hear, can you imagine how they might be for someone else?

2. Do you have any personal experience with the purity movement? Have you seen any damage caused by what could have been perceived as a works-righteousness message from that era of evangelicalism? What's the potential fallout when we trade a relationship with God and living for his glory for the lesser gods of a good marriage, great sex, and great kids?

3. Have you ever considered how both Jesus and the apostle Paul were single? What do you think about Jesus saying, "Let the one who

is able to receive this receive it" (Matt. 19:12) and Paul saying, "I wish that all were as I myself am" (1 Cor. 7:7)?

4. Reflect on the two covenants and a commission. How is God's covenant with Abraham similar to and different from his new covenant through Jesus? How are Israel and the church the same and different? Read Matthew 28:19–20 and talk about how the Great Commission is a sort of crown atop the covenants.

5. Do you prioritize your family in Christ? Do you make time to be with your brothers and sisters in the church? Or do you tend to stay isolated from others in your church? What might it look like to be more inclusive of your spiritual siblings in your day-to-day?

6. Do you struggle with wanting the blessings of the Father but not a relationship with the Father? Read Luke 15:31, and close by thanking God for this truth and asking him to open your eyes to it more and more.

PART 3

WE WERE MADE FOR
SO MUCH MORE

Truly our God is the giver of life. He is for us. His design of women and girls is good. Our role in his grand story is eternal and glorious because he is. Part 3 is full of the good news we have in Jesus, our kind Creator and Savior. No matter what we've done, no matter what our world is like, no matter what happens, our Father is with us and offers all that he has to us.

The thief comes only to steal and kill and destroy. I came that they may have life and have it abundantly. I am the good shepherd. The good shepherd lays down his life for the sheep. He who is a hired hand and not a shepherd, who does not own the sheep, sees the wolf coming and leaves the sheep and flees, and the wolf snatches them and scatters them. He flees because he is a hired hand and cares nothing for the sheep. I am the good shepherd. I know my own and my own know me, just as the Father knows me and I know the Father; and I lay down my life for the sheep. (John 10:10–15)

9

It's Good to Be a Girl

WHEN I LOOKED AROUND my church one recent Sunday, I saw what the vast majority of churches bear witness to every week: more women than men. You know from our historical jaunt in chapter 2 that the Christian church has always been majority female. It's ironic, because the secular world frames Christianity as sexist, when, in fact, Jesus and his church have always been unapologetically pro-female.

The evangelical Protestant church in the United States is currently 55 percent female and 45 percent male.[1] When I tell my friends these statistics and historical realities, they are always shocked.

There is a gnawing, often unspoken, idea that boys have it better than girls. Granted, we have just explored five idols in the Western world that have been especially destructive to women and girls. When it comes to outward beauty and ability, hooking up, abortion, gender and sexuality, and marriage and motherhood, women and girls *do* face a unique set of cultural circumstances that our

1   "Gender Composition," in Religious Landscape Study, Pew Research Center, accessed July 2020, https://www.pewforum.org.

brothers do not face. The disparities we uncovered in part 2 are not imagined. However, the inherent dignity, the intrinsic value, and the worth of a woman are not less than a man's. We are wonderfully made (Ps. 139:14).

This is no attempt to trumpet girl power or to deny the immeasurable goodness of our brothers. This is a heralding of what's true: girlhood is good. This truth is worth examining and expressing because, as I covered in chapter 2, second-wave feminism declared that in order to be equal to men, women had to be the *same* as men. Rather than rejoicing over the uniqueness of women, the male body and male roles were normed. That was a deadly miscalculation.

We in the church should be the loudest voice in our world to rehearse all the ways it's good to be a girl. We know the God who made us, and we know he made us very good. Expressing this truth should be a top priority for us, as it directly pertains to more than half the church.

Why is it good to be a girl? Here are ten answers to that question.

Created by God

The first reason it's good to be a girl is that we are created by a good, beautiful, and true God. He is merciful and relational, and he delights in you and me. Because we live in a culture that insists we are self-made, it's worth repeating that we are creatures with a Creator. Remembering and realigning ourselves to the truth that we are God-made is a necessary spiritual discipline in the twenty-first century.

Without this foundational truth, everything else goes awry. If you and I cannot admit and rejoice in the reality that our lives have an author, then we will never fully thrive. The abundant life comes through Jesus, and only Jesus (John 10:10).

In her poem *"What Is a Woman?"* Jackie Hill Perry says, "If you asked me, 'What is a woman?' I would simply tell you, 'Ask God who made her.'"[2] When we seek to understand who we are, we must always remember *whose* we are.

And knowing *whose* we are is very good news indeed.

Created to Image God

The second reason it's good to be a girl is that we are created in the image of our good God. We are *imago dei*, created to reflect him, to take after him. In her book *In His Image*, Bible teacher Jen Wilkin shares ten ways God calls us to reflect his character: "God is holy, loving, just, good, merciful, gracious, faithful, truthful, patient, and wise."[3] Of course, we will never fully image these attributes, because we are not sinless, as God is.

But as the saying goes, like Father, like daughter. We thrive when we walk in his design.

There is no greater source of dignity or joy or worth than to be created *imago dei*. The almighty Creator of the universe made us female to take after him. This was his doing, his design, his good plan. Women are not afterthoughts, or second best, or evolutionary by-products. Our good God set out with intention, knowing his image was not complete in Adam alone, to make you and me.

Created for Community

The third reason it's good to be a girl is that we were made for community. After the Lord God created Adam from dust and

2 Jackie Hill Perry, "The Truth about Ourselves," session transcript, *Revive Our Hearts*, September 27, 2018, https://www.reviveourhearts.com/.

3 Jen Wilkin, *In His Image: 10 Ways God Calls Us to Reflect His Character* (Wheaton: Crossway, 2018), 22.

breathed his own breath into the man's nostrils, he declared it was not good for Adam to be alone. Eve was made from Adam's rib, and God commanded the two to be fruitful and multiply. Just as our God lives in community—the Trinity—so he created us to live in community.

In our self-focused and fiercely individualistic age, it's another necessary spiritual discipline to remember that we were not created for ourselves but for one another. Author Wendy Alsup says from the "earliest words of God over humanity, we see that even in perfection, one by himself could not attain the full good that God intended for him. God's vision for our good is communal. . . . The flourishing of communities is necessary for the flourishing of the individual."[4]

Our thriving depends on our living in light of each other. This truth is what differentiates first-wave feminism from second-wave feminism. In the first wave, women were concerned about the well-being of society. They faced down multiple evils: slavery, inhumane working conditions in urban centers, strong drink, and the all-too-common abuse of women and children. They marched for the vote and to own property so they could protect one another, protect their children, and raise the quality of life for all who were marginalized. In the second wave, though, women protested not for communal flourishing but for individual autonomy. The cry of the second wave was *my* body, *my* choice.

It is good for women—and for everyone—when we live in light of each other. We were made to have compassionate hearts, to display kindness, humility, meekness, and patience, and to bear with one another in love (Col. 3:12–13). This is our calling. This is our true composition as God's creatures.

4 Wendy Alsup, *Is the Bible Good for Women? Seeking Clarity and Confidence through a Jesus-Centered Understanding of Scripture* (Colorado Springs: Multnomah, 2017), 85.

Created with a Unique Calling

The fourth reason it's good to be a girl is we have a unique and compelling calling. Right after the Lord said, "It is not good that the man should be alone," he said, "I will make him a helper fit for him" (Gen. 2:18). Our twenty-first-century sensibilities bristle immediately at the word *helper*. Helper feels so secondary, like Adam needed an assistant—someone to take care of the inconsequential stuff.

The original language and biblical context of Eve's creation should shape how we view our gender and our design. The word for helper is *ezer* in the original Hebrew language. *Ezer* shows up twenty-one times in the Old Testament, including sixteen times as a description of God himself.[5] Obviously, our God is not secondary, nor is he inconsequential.

Here is just a sampling of the use of *ezer* in the Old Testament:

- "Happy are you, O Israel! Who is like you, / a people saved by the Lord, / the shield of your *help*, / and the sword of your triumph!" (Deut. 33:29)
- "Our soul waits for the Lord; / he is our *help* and our shield." (Ps. 33:20)
- "But I am poor and needy; / hasten to me, O God! / You are my *help* and my deliverer; / O Lord, do not delay!" (Ps. 70:5)
- "Israel, trust in the Lord! / He is their *help* and their shield. / O house of Aaron, trust in the Lord! / He is their *help* and their shield. / You who fear the Lord, trust in the Lord! / He is their *help* and their shield." (Ps. 115:9–11)

---

5 "'ezer," *Bible Study Tools*, accessed July 2020, https://www.biblestudytools.com/lexicons/hebrew/nas/ezer-2.html.

- "I lift up my eyes to the hills. / From where does my *help* come? / My *help* comes from the LORD, / who made heaven and earth." (Ps. 121:1–2)

Ezer is associated with shields, swords, triumph, delivery, comfort, and awe. As Alsup points out, "God, sovereign Lord of the universe, is our helper, and He created woman to reflect this aspect of Him. If we hold on to the dominant cultural attitude that being a helper is a substandard identity, we mock the name of God and his character. The role of helper is one he willingly embraces."[6]

Whether in our homes, neighborhoods, workplaces, churches, or anywhere else, we are meant to be protectors, deliverers, shields, comforters—a help to those God has placed with us. It's hard to imagine a more dignified calling or a more exciting role for us in creation.

Look around you right now—who can you help? Who needs your protection and care? Who can you defend or triumph? Who can you comfort? This is your calling. Walk in it.

Created for Redemption

The fifth reason it's good to be a girl is that we are redeemed. Through the work of our Savior, "the gospel . . . *re-images* us."[7] While the Lord's image in us was marred by the fall, it is *re-imaged* in us through Jesus. When you and I surrender to the love and mercy of Jesus Christ, he begins to transform us from the inside out, and we become a new creation (2 Cor. 5:17).

Jesus, our rescuer and Redeemer, paves the way to our restoration. There is no greater love, no greater mercy, no better gift. We

---

6 Alsup, *Is the Bible Good for Women?*, 48–49.
7 Wilkin, *In His Image*, 14.

are not alienated forever from the God who made us. Instead, Jesus came low to serve (to help!) you and me.

In *What Is a Woman?* Hill Perry says, "They say, 'Submission sounds like servant.' They say, 'That sounds like something to rebel against.' I say, 'Ain't it funny that servant is repulsive to everyone but God?' And we wonder why we can't recognize His face."[8] When we bristle at the idea of serving and helping, we bristle at the very character of our God.

Jesus came "not to be served but to serve, and to give his life as a ransom for many" (Matt. 20:28). You can see his kindness and servant's heart toward women in countless stories. He took notice of a poor widow and made an example of her faith and generosity (Mark 12:41–44). He healed a woman with a disability in the synagogue on the Sabbath (Luke 13:10–17). He healed several women from evil spirits and infirmities including Mary Magdalene, Joanna, Susanna, and many others, who in turn provided for Jesus and his disciples out of their own means (Luke 8:2–3). With compassion, Jesus touched and healed the woman who had suffered from a bleeding disorder for twelve years, calling her "daughter" (Mark 5:34). He took the little girl Talitha by the hand and raised her from the dead (Mark 5:41). He initiated a conversation full of grace and truth across ethnic lines with the Samaritan adulteress at the well and offered her living water (John 4:1–30).

What we see in Jesus is not only the God who made us and the rescuer who saves us, but also the kind and compassionate teacher who leads us. As the redeemed, we increasingly *re-image* Jesus to a watching world, serving others that they may come to know him too.

---

8 Jackie Hill Perry, "The Truth about Ourselves," session transcript, *Revive Our Hearts*, September 27, 2018, https://www.reviveourhearts.com/.

Created to Reconcile

The sixth reason it's good to be a girl is that we have a holy mission before us. We are in that already-but-not-yet place in history. Christ has already come and brought redemption, but he has not yet returned, so we await restoration. But as we wait, we have a calling, a sacred vocation.

In this already-but-not-yet time we are called to "go therefore and make disciples of all nations, baptizing them in the name of the Father and of the Son and of the Holy Spirit, teaching them to observe all that [Jesus has commanded us]" (Matt. 28:19–20). We are to be Jesus's "witnesses in Jerusalem and in all Judea and Samaria, and to the end of the earth" (Acts 1:8). We are called to be ambassadors of Christ, imploring others to be reconciled to our good God (2 Cor. 5:20).

We women are as diverse as our God is creative. Our ministries vary as much as our hair color, body type, and style preferences. But we must all love God and love others by *going and telling*. The Christian life is meant to be an adventure, a joy, a faith-requiring endeavor. Without faith it is impossible to please God (Heb. 11:6).

To be a Christian girl or woman is to be called to have great faith and to do hard things. That may be in your living room or it may be in a land overseas—but either way your vocation is far from ho-hum. Where are you pursuing your ministry of reconciliation? Who are you telling about the love and mercy of Jesus?

The Sisters before Us

The seventh reason it's good to be a girl is we have a multitude of examples of God-fearing, God-loving, God-honoring women who have gone before us. Their stories are recorded in Scripture and remind us that while our lives are brief, God's work in us is eternal.

We are threads in his hands, as he weaves the beautiful tapestry of his kingdom across time and space.

God works through all kinds of personalities and circumstances. Think of Eve. She was marked by shame after eating the fruit but was still used of God. She became the mother of all the living (Gen. 3:20) and was given the promise that her offspring would ultimately bruise the head of the serpent (Gen. 3:15). Eve's story is a declaration that no matter what a woman has done, she remains precious and useful to the Lord.

Or there's Sarah, who was old and barren and yet conceived and gave birth to Isaac. She teaches us that God can do the impossible and use us for his purposes, even when we disbelieve and even when we think we are physically incapable (Gen. 21). And further on in the Old Testament I'm moved by Deborah, Israel's strong and godly leader (Judg. 4), and Jael, the Israelite woman who killed an enemy by driving a tent peg through his temple (Judg. 4), and Ruth, who was devoted to her mother-in-law and became the great-grandmother of King David (Ruth 1–4). I could go on about Rahab, Hannah, Abigail, Bathsheba, Esther, and many others.

The New Testament gives us Jesus's own biological mother, Mary, who said, "I am the servant of the Lord; let it be to me according to your word" (Luke 1:38). Anna, the eighty-four-year-old prophetess and widow, blessed the baby Jesus in the temple after waiting for his arrival for many decades while worshiping, fasting, and praying day and night (Luke 2). There's Tabitha, a woman full of good works and acts of charity (Acts 9), Mary and Lydia, who supported and hosted the early church (Acts 12, 16), and so many more women listed in Paul's letters who proclaimed Christ and served the church.

We have many awe-inspiring examples of imperfect women—many in unspeakably difficult circumstances—who served our perfect God before us. May their names rise in your heart with a crescendo: *Look how good it has always been to be a girl.* God loves us, makes us his own, and uses us for his glory and the good of his people.

The Sisters Next to Us

The eighth reason it's good to be a girl is there are countless ways we can be *ezers* here and now, for God's glory and for the flourishing of our communities. Like the long list of women above, we each live in a unique time and place, and everything we have and experience, even down to the breath in our lungs, is a gift and purposefully designed by God (Acts 17:25–26).

This is an exciting time to be alive. As redeemed saints, we await our Savior. As women in the twenty-first century, we have access to myriad resources. How will you combine your holy calling with all that you have? How will you steward the resources and place God has you to care for his creation and proclaim his goodness? In what specific way will you go and tell others about him?

I am inspired and spurred on by many friends. My friend Robin leverages her current calling to singleness on the mission field by sharing Christ with neighbors who come from all corners of the globe to her urban metropolis. My friend Sandra uses her education and wisdom to care for marginalized students in one of our nation's most diverse and impoverished communities. My friend Kate is an adoptive mom with a household of children with special needs. Kara proclaims Christ in her role in state politics. Laurie is an ambassador for Jesus around her kitchen table, as she daily tells her preschool-aged children about Jesus. Naomi is a Muslimbackground follower of Jesus who relentlessly shares the gospel with her mom. Sherry and her husband are empty nesters who opened an orphanage overseas. Brenda (my mom!) teaches English to newly arrived refugees. And my friend Sarah repeats the gospel over and over by faith to her mom, who lives in a nursing home.

It's good to be a girl because we are not called to a run-of-the-mill Western lifestyle. We were not made for the safety, security, comfort, and ease of the American dream. Anything we do, in the name of the Lord Jesus for his glory and the good of others, is a divine adventure.

These women remind me that we were made for the abundant life in Christ.

The Sisters Coming Up after Us

The ninth reason it's good to be a girl is that we get to proclaim the goodness of our God to the girls coming up after us. It's our voice that will shape the next generation.

My husband and I have heard "It's a girl!" three times, and we adopted one more, making a total of four little women in our home. Mark's favorite joke is to say he's in full-time women's ministry. But honestly, he is. And so am I. And so are you, if you know any little girls. It's one thing to *be* a girl. It's another thing altogether to raise them. I've never wanted to get anything so right in my life.

You and I have the privilege of reading through the pages of God's word and satisfying our souls with a feast of grace and truth. In those pages we see God's grand story, and we find the stories of other women woven through. We also find our own story, and we find our daughters' stories as well.

We are part of a spiritual lineage, the genealogy of God's people. Just like the women above who lived in Bible times, we and the girls after us are generations in God's eternal family.

We Will Prosper

And finally, the tenth reason it's good to be a girl is that our God will ensure that we prosper. In part 2 we looked at five winsome counterfeits of our age—five promises our world makes to women about who they should be. These promises, as we saw, do not deliver. Each one has a pretty facade but a rotten core. Each one promises life but falls woefully short. When depended upon for meaning, value, and identity, we crush them and they crush us.

But throughout Scripture we see a promise that those who belong to the Lord will prosper. Psalm 1 instructs us to not listen to the wicked, the sinners, and the scoffers (Ps. 1:1), but delight instead in God and his word. Our God who dwells within us will make you and me like trees planted by streams of water. As we abide in him, we will yield fruit in season, and our leaves will not wither. All that we do will prosper (Ps. 1:2–3).

In God's presence there is fullness of joy (Ps. 16:11), life abundant and everlasting (John 10:10, 28). Let's reject the empty promises of our age and embrace instead the God who satisfies our longing souls and fills you and me with good things (Ps. 107:9).

This really is the best story—we were made for so much more.

Discussion Questions

1. Have you had a gnawing, unspoken idea that boys have it better than girls (when it comes to God or life or anything)? How does the reality that there are more Christian women than men affect your thinking?

2. What do you think about the Hebrew word *ezer*? Reread the Old Testament verses on page 175–76 where *ezer* describes God. How

does this definition shape your understanding of our calling as women? Does that align with what you've been taught before, both inside and outside the church? Where are you currently exercising your calling as an *ezer*?

3. The Christian life is meant to be an adventure, a joy, and a faith-requiring endeavor. Without faith it is impossible to please God (Heb. 11:6). Is there anything you're doing right now that requires faith?

4. Look through the women in the Bible mentioned above, starting with Eve and ending with all the women Paul addresses in his letters. Pick a couple favorite stories and encourage one another by telling each other why you're drawn to those particular women.

5. We women and girls are part of a spiritual lineage, the genealogy of God's people. Just like the women above who lived in Bible times, we and the girls after us are links in God's eternal family. How would you express this truth to a biological or spiritual daughter of yours? What truths would you want her to know?

6. Close by reading Psalm 1. Pray and ask the Lord to help you delight in his word and not listen to those in the world who do not know him, his will for women, or why it's really good to be a girl.

10

Home

WE HAVE A SIGN HANGING over our dining room table that reads, "There will always, always be a place for you at My table."[1] It's a line from a song by Josh Garrels on his album *Home*. In the song he retells the story of the Prodigal Son, and in the chorus the Father beckons his wayward child home, promising a joyful and warm embrace and a place at his table.

I made the sign myself when we moved back to the United States for the first time after many years overseas. Just months prior, Garrels's album was on repeat while our family drove from Budapest through Bratislava and into Brno, which was "home" at the time. Our dear and young friend in California was dying from cancer, and we were rushing from a conference to the airport to get back for his funeral, which my husband would officiate. At the same time, we suspected our trip "home" would be a semipermanent relocation, because my dad, who was ailing from Alzheimer's and dementia, needed our care. The soulful *Home* became the soundtrack of our lives.

1   Josh Garrels, "At the Table," track 1 on *Home*, Mason Jar Music and Josh Garrels, 2015, digital album.

Home, where Drew would go after his battle with cancer. *Home*, where my dad lived and needed me. *Home*, in Europe at the time, but in Asia for many years before that, and in the United States next. *Home*. It can be elusive.

The sign helps all of us Oshmans remember that *home* is at our Father's table. He invites us in, unconditionally, joyfully, and always. The sign challenges me to walk in my Father's footsteps, to be ever ready for anybody to take a seat at our table. I want my children to know that their earthly parents as well as their Father in heaven will always, always have a place for them at the table. I want all who enter our home to know they have a place here.

I want to remember that *home* is where my Father is.

East of Eden

We humans have been looking and longing for home ever since our first parents had to leave the garden of Eden. When Adam and Eve disobeyed the Lord, he "sent [them] out from the garden of Eden to work the ground from which [Adam] was taken . . . and at the east of the garden of Eden he placed the cherubim and a flaming sword that turned every way to guard the way to the tree of life" (Gen. 3:23–24).

We've been east of Eden ever since. Away from home and trying to get back.

In chapter 1 we looked at two stories that tend to run around in everyone's head. The two stories speak to our desire for home, for peace, for that deep-down knowing that you are right where you're supposed to be.

The first story is proclaimed loudly throughout popular culture. It's the narrative of advertisements, movies and songs, social media influencers, and even the laws of our land. The first story says you are the center of the universe and you can be awesome. You just have to make it happen.

This first story is what peddles the counterfeits in this book. We're conditioned and convinced to think that our lives are worth less if we aren't beautiful enough or able enough, or that soul-deep satisfaction will come through being sexy or having just one more sexual encounter. That first story says you and I must have the choice to eliminate our babies if they're not part of our plan, or to be a different gender, or to seek peace in the arms of another lover. The first story says you'll find fulfillment as soon as you get married, or become a mom, or whatever. The first story implores us to make ourselves in any image we desire. It convinces us that the good life is the culmination of you and me making just the right series of life decisions.

These decisions usually go one of two directions, and we see them both in the story of the prodigal son and his older brother. In the former it's license and in the latter it's legalism. The prodigal brother takes his father's money and runs to a far country, seeking to be awesome through reckless living. The older brother stays home on his father's estate and lives morally and carefully, seeking the good life through strict obedience. As we saw in chapter 8, both brothers wanted the father's gifts, but not the father. Neither brother was after his dad's love and companionship. Rather, both pursued their own vision of the good life, and in both cases they came up short. The younger brother's reckless living led to his downfall. And the older brother's pride in his own perfection led to his.

I think most of us can see ourselves in both brothers—maybe one more than the other. Looking at my own life, I can see plenty of both license and legalism. Sometimes in the span of a single day I will put hope in sin to deliver me and then I will put hope in my own good efforts to deliver me. Believing that first story in my head—*I can be awesome, I just have to make it happen*—I can swing wildly from *forget it all* to *clench it all* in just a few minutes.

But there's that second story in our heads too. It's the quiet whisper that beckons us home. That second story insists there must be more to this life, but we so often shush it with our frantic pace. Chasing the first story, we silence the second. Until one day, when we can't run anymore. Burned out, we either come to ourselves out in the far country, or we come to the realization that no matter how many perfect choices we make, they simply don't satisfy.

Neither pursuing the fast life of the flesh nor pursuing our own prideful perfection delivers the deep peace we were made for. The younger brother woke up hungry, exhausted, and needy. The older brother flew into an angry, entitled rage. Both brothers came up against the truth that there *must be more to this life.*

In our age we often call it *burnout*—it's a coming to the end of ourselves. It's when we hit rock bottom, beat up from doing life our own way, on our own terms. Burnout is painful, for sure. But it's a gift of grace. It's the first step in our journey home. No more trusting in the empty promises of our age. No more giving ourselves over to fake identities or self-reliant living. We wave our white flags and surrender to the good God who made us and died to save us.

The Father Runs Out to His Lost Son

Defeated by poverty, starvation, and alienation in a far country, the Prodigal Son finally comes to himself and devises a plan. He is sure he cannot reenter his family estate as a son. Those rights have been lost forever. But to even be a hired servant to his father would be a better fate than longing for pig's food. He determines to go home and say, "I am no longer worthy to be called your son. Treat me as one of your hired servants" (Luke 15:19). In the son's mind, he can at least pay his father to be fed and sheltered again.

Maybe you see yourself here, awakening to the truth that you've prized your outward appearance above the heart, or you're ashamed of your sexual sin or your abortion or your same-sex attraction. You're wondering how you can ever get your act together so that you can finally come home. Know this: our God loves you and is watching intently, just waiting for you to turn to him.

You can head home this very minute.

"But while he was still a long way off, his father saw him" (Luke 15:20). The father had been watching, routinely squinting at the distant road and direction toward which his son had left months, or maybe even years, before. He never stopped looking and hoping for his son's return—his son, who had essentially wished the father dead when he prematurely requested his inheritance before he headed off on his doomed journey.

"His father saw him and felt compassion, and ran and embraced him and kissed him" (Luke 15:20). This scene is touching to us in the twenty-first century, but to ancient Middle Eastern ears it would have been downright scandalous. The hearers would have expected to hear about the father's vehement and maybe violent rejection of his wayward boy. The son would have endured extreme humiliation even as he walked through the village back home, because everyone would have known his mortifying misdeeds when he left. But, driven by compassion, the father runs out and *takes upon himself the humiliation due the Prodigal.*

Kenneth Bailey is a well-known author and expert on the New Testament and the Middle East, as he lived there for forty years. In his book *The Cross and the Prodigal* he says the word *ran* that

WE WERE MADE FOR SO MUCH MORE

Luke uses here is the word used for racing.[2] The father doesn't jog to his boy; he races. Bailey says, "In the Middle East a man of his age and position *always* walks in a slow, dignified fashion. . . . But now the father races down the road. To do so he must take the front edge of his robes in his hand like a teenager . . . his legs show in what is considered a humiliating posture. All of this is painfully shameful for him."[3]

Is this not a picture of Immanuel, God with us? This is the incarnation on display. The father willingly left his honor, his wealth, and his security and humiliated himself to run to his son. This is the same willing humiliation we see in Jesus in Philippians 2:5–8: "Christ Jesus, who, though he was in the form of God, did not count equality with God a thing to be grasped, but emptied himself, by taking the form of a servant, being born in the likeness of men. And being found in human form, he humbled himself by becoming obedient to the point of death, even death on a cross."

The Prodigal begins to say to his father, "I have sinned against heaven and before you. I am no longer worthy to be called your son" (Luke 15:21). But before he goes on with his prior plan to become a hired servant, the father starts telling his servants to prepare a lavish party. He says, "'For this my son was dead, and is alive again; he was lost, and is found.' And they began to celebrate" (Luke 15:24).

The father knows there's no way his son can repay him. He can never earn a place back in his household. Both father and son are well aware that the Prodigal deserves to be disowned, rejected, and cast out forever. The father's compassion and kindness lead to the

---

2   Kenneth E. Bailey, *The Cross and the Prodigal: Luke 15 through the Eyes of Middle Eastern Peasants* (Downers Grove, IL: InterVarsity Press, 2005), 67.
3   Bailey, *The Cross and the Prodigal*, 67.

son's brokenness and genuine repentance. The son understands no plan he devises can make a way to fix the broken divide.

And the father doesn't say, "Go get cleaned up and we'll talk." In his limitless love and matchless mercy, the father clothes the son in his best robe—he covers his boy in his own righteousness. The son's name is restored with the father's ring. His bare, orphan feet are covered in shoes. The father reestablishes the son's position in the community by inviting everyone to come and celebrate his return. The son is totally unworthy of this public display of honor and love. But he receives it nonetheless, because his father is so good, so kind, so willing to take shame upon himself so that he and his boy might be reconciled. It's irresistible grace.

The Prodigal is free now to relate to his father as a dearly loved son. He doesn't have to operate from a place of fear or worry that he will be cast out or never measure up. He doesn't have to impress his father or neighbors to earn back his position. He has been fully reconciled and can now be moved by love and gratitude alone. There is no way for you or me to repay our Father. There is nothing we can do to make him love us more or love us less. His love and forgiveness are complete and unconditional. May his kindness lead us to repentance.

The Father Entreats the Older Brother

Understandably, the big brother is angry. If you have a sibling or have ever been in a classroom with a wayward classmate, you know the feeling. *Ugh. This guy! I follow the rules perfectly, but he ruins everything for everyone. What a fool.* It's not hard to fathom how the hatred grows, because we've all felt those seeds at one time or another. None of us are immune to thinking we are better people, more deserving, more entitled.

Bailey gives us a clue that even before the Prodigal set out for the far country, all was not right between the older brother and the father, as well as the older brother and the younger brother. We don't pick up on these details in our Western context, but Bailey says it would have been obvious in the East that the older brother was required to mediate between the younger brother and their father. However, "he refuses to fulfill the sacred responsibility that village custom places on his shoulders. Clearly, for some reason he does not want reconciliation to take place . . . the refusal is a clear indication of his broken relationship with his father."[4]

When the older brother hears the happy celebration taking place, he comes in from the fields and asks the servants what's going on. They tell him, "Your brother has come, and your father has killed the fattened calf, because he has received him back safe and sound" (Luke 15:27). In his anger the older brother refuses to go in to the party. Again, our Western understanding falls short. But in the East, "the male members of the family must come and shake hands with the guests. . . . Failure to fulfill this courtesy is a personal insult to the guests and to the father, as host."[5] The older brother's refusal to go in is a blatant and public act of rebellion against his father. The villagers see it happen and understand that the older son is willing to rupture his relationship with his father. To us it may seem like a mere sulking in the corner, but to them this deserves harsh and swift discipline or rejection from the father.

Instead, once again, we see the limitless compassion of the father. For the second time that day he goes out to a wayward son. For the second time that day he takes upon himself the public shame and humiliation due to his boy in order to reconcile with

4 Bailey, *The Cross and the Prodigal*, 45.
5 Bailey, *The Cross and the Prodigal*, 82.

him. The father pays the price. He entreats, rather than rejects (Luke 15:28).

In the face of boundless mercy and love, the son is bitter and enraged. "Look, these many years I have served you, and I never disobeyed your command, yet you never gave me a young goat, that I might celebrate with my friends. But when this son of yours came, who has devoured your property with prostitutes, you killed the fattened calf for him!" (Luke 15:29–30). His focus is on his work for the father. He doesn't see himself as a son, but as a worker, earning his pay. His focus is on the law—he's keeping score, and in his estimation his perfection has earned him nothing, while his brother's bad behavior has earned him everything. We see plainly that the older brother's motives have been self-focused all along. He has never been motivated by love for his father.

Maybe you see yourself here, angry and embittered because you've done all the right things and made all the right choices. You stayed pure. You married a man in the church. You birthed those babies with all the expected outcomes that your good behavior warrants. Or you've behaved just so, and nothing has gone right. No marriage, no motherhood, none of the blessings you've been waiting for. Your heart cries out to the Lord, *Look, I've served you all these years, and what have you given me?*

Remember, Jesus's audience for this story is the Pharisees, who believe that blessing and salvation came through obedience to the Scriptures. He's talking to a crowd of older brothers, and we can be sure they are well aware that Jesus means for them to see themselves here. Jesus entreats them when he gives voice to the father, "Son, you are always with me, and all that is mine is yours" (Luke 15:31). Identifying with the father, Jesus invites them to repent and receive all his good gifts that he's always had and always wanted to lavish on them. Our Savior extends grace to even the most religious, and the most moral. They need it too. If you, like the Pharisees, have believed that salvation comes through your obedience, the Father says now to you too, *All that is mine is yours. Come to me.*

The True Older Brother

The Pharisees listening in know that the older brother in this story has failed in his calling to care for his younger brother. They know he should have been involved from the beginning—begging the Prodigal not to leave, doing everything in his power to bring him home and restore him to the family. They are well aware that older brothers are, in fact, required to be their brothers' keepers (Gen. 4:9).

Not only does Jesus want the Pharisees to see that hoping in their own righteousness will lead to a bitter dead end, but he also wants them to wonder why the older brother hasn't properly carried out this part of his role. Tim Keller says, "By putting a flawed elder brother in the story, Jesus is inviting us to imagine and yearn for a true one."[6]

And we have a true older brother. He's Jesus. He's our mediator (1 Tim. 2:5). He is not ashamed to call you and me brothers and sisters (Heb. 2:11). He is the firstborn among us (Rom. 8:29). Jesus is your true older brother, and mine.

Jesus did not just go to a far country to pursue you and me. He left heaven, put on flesh, and walked this earth in a search and rescue mission. And it cost him everything. Jesus took the price of our reconciliation upon himself and paid our way with his life. He endured the public humiliation that we deserve. He hung naked,

6 Timothy Keller, *Prodigal God: Recovering the Heart of the Christian Faith* (New York: Dutton, 2008), 84.

stripped of dignity, stature, and clothing. He wrapped us in his own robes of salvation and righteousness (Isa. 61:10).

Oh, what a Savior. Oh, what a King. Our big brother is good beyond our wildest imaginings.

Jesus saw our hopeless estate and came down. Whether we are more of a Prodigal or more of an older brother—whether we search for meaning, significance, and identity in reckless living or in our own righteous behavior—Jesus sees and intervenes. He is not ashamed of us, but runs to us and reconciles us to the Father through the cross.

Whatever you have done, wherever you have gone, Jesus stands ready to forgive you, as you receive him. He already paid the price in full to bring you all the way home. "There is therefore now no condemnation for those who are in Christ Jesus" (Rom. 8:1).

His life for your death. The cross is enough. "If the Son sets you free, you will be free indeed" (John 8:36).

Because of our good older brother, we are adopted sons and daughters (Gal. 4:5). We get to say "Abba! Father!" to our God in heaven (4:6). We are no longer slaves, but children, heirs through Jesus (4:7). We no longer have to search for the good life in reckless living or in our own good behavior. Our efforts fall short, but Jesus's do not. As we behold our Savior, the chains of both ways of life are loosened. As we behold his goodness, we break free from the empty promises of our age. Brothers and sisters, we can rest in the finished work of our real elder brother, Jesus. In him, we have so much more.

All That Was Lost Has Been Found

When our first parents had to leave Eden, we all lost so much. In our sinful state we've been looking and longing for home ever since. It's the human experience. We know we are exiles. We all know there must be more to this life. We are sure we were made for more.

In just our own lifetimes so much has been lost. I think of the havoc wreaked just since the Sexual Revolution. The *imago dei* has been disregarded—humans made in God's image and for his good purposes have been used and cast aside. Children have been sacrificed. Families have disintegrated. Fathers have left. God's creatures have misused each other. We've exploited each other for selfish gain.

God's image in us whispers *Yes, you were made for more*. Women who don't know they have a good older brother don red cloaks and white bonnets and march, seeking more, yearning for better treatment. There's an awareness amongst us in the West that women and girls deserve better. We cannot escape our Christian heritage. The goodness of the one true God toward women has shaped us. Because of the legacy of Jesus Christ, we know that abundant life must be out there somewhere.

It is. The Lord God above is leading all his children home even now. Jesus came to seek and to save the lost, and he is reconciling "to himself all things, whether on earth or in heaven, making peace by the blood of his cross" (Col. 1:20). Jesus is after the renewal and restoration of his creation. He is after "the end of disease, poverty, injustice, violence, suffering and death. The climax of history is . . . a feast."[7] Heaven awaits, and it's not boring. It's the biggest celebration ever, and there will be "music and dancing" (Luke 15:25), just like the older brother heard.

Even as we await heaven, we are invited to "taste and see that the LORD is good" (Ps. 34:8). As we await the feast of the Lamb, Jesus says *abide in me* (John 15:4), *come to me* (Matt. 11:28), *all things are possible through me* (Matt. 19:26).

---

7   Keller, *Prodigal God*, 110–11.

When Jesus began his ministry on earth, he entered the synagogue and read the words of the prophet Isaiah:

The Spirit of the Lord is upon me,
  because he has anointed me
  to proclaim good news to the poor.
He has sent me to proclaim liberty to the captives
  and recovering of sight to the blind,
  to set at liberty those who are oppressed,
to proclaim the year of the Lord's favor. (Luke 4:18–19)

Through Jesus we have *so much more* than we could have ever dreamed, so much more than we deserve.

Home is a person. His name is Jesus.

Human well-being requires harmony with reality. East of Eden, we've been seeking and striving after meaning and significance. Like the Prodigal, we've sought it out in a far country: outward beauty and ability, cheap sex, abortion, and changing identities on the LGBTQIA+ spectrum. But we've been left hungry, exhausted, and homeless by these empty promises of our age. Like the older brother, we've sought identity and peace through right behavior, exalting the good gifts of marriage and motherhood way beyond their rightful place. These empty promises have left us angry, disappointed, and unsatisfied because they haven't delivered what they said they would. We've missed out on harmony because we've rejected reality.

What's real is that we have a good God, and he stands ready to heal. King David said it well: "The sorrows of those who run after another god shall multiply" (Ps. 16:4). But in the Lord we "have a beautiful inheritance" (Ps. 16:6). It is our God in heaven who makes known to us the path of life. In his presence there is fullness of joy. It is he who gives us pleasures forevermore (Ps. 16:11).

Let's go home, friends. Life was meant to be so much more. A feast awaits. There will always, always be a place for us at our Father's table.

Discussion Questions

1. Start by rereading the parable of the prodigal son (Luke 15:11–32). In what ways do you identify with the Prodigal and in what ways do you identify with the older brother? Now that you've spent ten chapters thinking about both brothers and their different approaches to life, how do you view them differently than when you first started this book?

2. Reflect on the father's watching and running and embracing of the Prodigal when he returned home. Reflect on how the son had devised a plan to earn back his place on the estate, but never got a chance to verbalize it. List all the ways the father lavished love on the Prodigal. How does God's kindness and grace toward your licentiousness lead you personally to repentance?

3. Now turn your reflections to how the father responded to the older son. Reflect on the older brother's response to the feast. Have you ever felt like that? Think about how the father entreated him, rather than rejected him. List all the ways the father lavished his love on his older son. How does God's kindness and grace toward your legalism lead you personally to repentance?

4. The father says to his son, "All that is mine is yours" (Luke 15:31). What does that mean for you, as a child of your Father in heaven? What, exactly, is yours?

5. Read Romans 8:29, 1 Timothy 2:5, and Hebrews 2:11. What does it mean that Jesus is our brother and mediator? Why do we need a true older brother and mediator? How does he mediate for us? What do you think about how he says he's not ashamed to call you and me brothers and sisters?

6. Close by reading Psalm 16. Pray and praise God for your beautiful inheritance. Ask your heavenly Father to show you the path of life and to impart to you the fullness of joy that comes through a relationship with him alone.

General Index

Scripture Index

Also Available from Jen Oshman

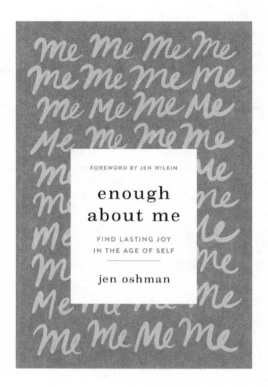

"Lord knows that we have more than enough books about ourselves and never enough books about the God that created us. It isn't until we see him that we can then make sense of ourselves. I believe Jen Oshman's book accomplishes that by widening our vision and helping us fall in love with seeing God again."

JACKIE HILL PERRY
poet; author; hip-hop artist

For more information, visit **crossway.org**.